GREED

What we all

Really need

To know

BY
JAMIE BEST

Copyright © 2024 Jamie Best

All rights reserved

Jamie Best
Little Dean
St Katherines Road
Torquay
Devon
TQ1 4DE

jbestchiefs@gmail.com

Full cover artwork and design by:

Mario Sánchez Nevado

https://marionevado.art

My thanks goes out to Mario, for his amazing artwork, and for all of his help in creating the full cover design of the book.

Thanks also goes to Ben Smith and Libby Bruten, for their offers of support in proof reading and preparing the book for publication.

Contents:

6 - **Introduction :** Why we all need to recognise the damage greed is doing.

14 - **Chapter 1 :** The human animal

22 - **Chapter 2 :** The pack mentality

30 - **Chapter 3 :** The alpha male, leadership and domination

40 - **Chapter 4 :** The growth of early human societies

48 - **Chapter 5 :** The historical spread of greed through war, imperialism and colonisations

59 - **Chapter 6 :** Social division, indoctrination and subjugation

79 - **Chapter 7 :** The industrial revolutions and modern imperialism

89 - **Chapter 8 :** Capitalism - the disguise and 'normalisation' of greed

98 - **Chapter 9 :** The black markets of greed

108 - **Chapter 10 :** The current state and challenges of the world that we have created:

    111- Resource control, exploitation of labour and inequality
    122- Advertising pressures and manipulation

129- Unsustainable economics and social instabilities
132- Modern wars and terrorism
134- Waste and pollution
145- Climate change
151- Resource depletion and rising populations
156- Environmental damage and falling wildlife populations

161 - **<u>Chapter 11 :</u>** Exploring the solutions to healing the disease

184 - **<u>Chapter 12 :</u>** A more intelligent human being

Introduction

When you really take the time to look at it in depth, this planet we live on is truly an amazing creation. According to radiometric dating and our subsequent scientific estimations, the Earth has been around and evolving for something over 4.5 billion years. Throughout that time it has been in constant movement, transition and evolution, passing through many different phases, eons and eras, each often lasting for many millions of years and then passing into the next.

The Earth first formed within a spiralling cloud of dust, integrated as the third planet within our solar system and in a fixed orbit around our sun, the central energy source to all life on Earth. How and why this came to be is a whole other debate, with both modern day human science and religion offering many different, off the shelf theories and stories as to how and why we came to exist here. However, to suggest it was all just accidental seems to lack any imagination; we can say we don't yet know the how and the why exactly, but when you really look at the overwhelming complexity and diversity of creation, just here on this planet, then it is impossible not to see some intelligence, direction and purpose in that creation. What that intelligence really is and where it comes from, is perhaps a quest that lies ahead for the human race; a more individual quest of genuine self-discovery that could eventually lead to collective realisations about how we have come into being and where we might continue to progress, in such a vast, and still unknown universe.

Every single one of us alive today, contains within us the entire spectrum of our evolution to date: from a single cell origin, through the many pathways of our growth and evolution, right up to our currently progressing threshold as modern human beings.

Each one of us is a multifaceted, highly complex, ego centred form of individual consciousness, living through an amazingly complex, self-regulating, physical organism: our human body. Within us and living through us are the systems and impulses of millions of years of evolution on this planet, and we all, if we so choose, now have the potential to consciously interact with those impulses, and to direct how we express and progress them in our own unique individual timelines of evolution.

And so, on to the premise of this particular book, which looks to examine a more indisputable fact now presenting our species with perhaps its greatest ever set of challenges to date. This book will look to establish the evidence, that Greed is a very real psychological human disease and imbalance, and that it is and has been more prevalent and more destructive than any other disease in human history. It currently has control of most of our world's resources and economies, and if we do not begin to find a way to turn this disease around and to heal and evolve beyond it, then it could, in reality, bring about our own self-destruction and mass extinction event.

Now the type of greed I am talking about is not just the small selfish instinct that might reach out and take the last piece of cake on the plate, even though the belly is full and others may not have had the opportunity to have some. The extremes of greed that I am referring to are a fully committed narcissistic and obsessive psychological imbalance, like a dark growing cancer within the human mind. This is the type of greed behind nearly all inflicted human suffering, war and environmental destruction: the type that looks to colonise and enslave populations; the type that looks to subjugate and control people and resources for one's own prosperity; the type that looks to justify and indoctrinate the inequality between the insanely rich and the impoverished, as something that is acceptable, even normal; and the type that would become so obsessed with personal wealth and power, that it would continually seek to carve apart and destroy large areas of the planet, just to fuel an ever increasing number of production lines aimed primarily at personal profiteering.

This type of greed, this disease, has been a growing disturbing fact and reality in our human world, becoming ever more exposed in our violent and primitive history of ruling classes, wars, invasions and colonisations. And it has evolved to become ever more established in our modern day capitalist world, exposed in the extreme realities of global impoverished slave labour, over production and waste, environmental destruction, rapid species extinctions, and long unregulated industrialised pollutions. These imbalances have all now begun to affect our climates to such a degree, that natural cycles and weather patterns are being hugely disturbed, causing the Earth's ability to continue to provide sustainably for us to be very much under threat.

Taken in and lead down the path of greed, no matter how much we might try to believe the political rhetoric that things are ok, that something will put this right eventually, we have, in reality, created an absolute mess of this planet. For decades now, centuries even, the mess has just been ignored and been swept under the carpet, and the general populations kept occupied and hidden from the true facts, until the very last minute that they can no longer be avoided. This is where we are now finding ourselves as a race today. The lump under the carpet has grown bigger than any mountain on Earth and we simply have no more space and time to continue avoiding it, so it must be faced up to in its entirety. The truths as to what greed has done and is still doing to our planet and to our social systems that control our life essential resources, are now out there for all to see, if you choose to really look with open eyes. The simple fact is, that solely responsible for this catastrophic mess and destruction, that we as a race have put upon ourselves and this planet, is the ignorance caused by the cancer and disease of human greed.

There may be some people among us who might wish to dispute this as a fact, and to defend the destructiveness of greed and its current forms of capitalist control over our resources and lives, suggesting that it is everyone's right to generate wealth and profit. But what I aim to do through this book is to take you on a revealing journey, from the simple origins of our animal nature and the fear that is an innate instinct within all humans, through the ages of our recorded history and greed's spread and expansion through indoctrination, wars, slavery and colonisations, right up to the present, and greed's hold on most of our modern day political and economic thinking, enabling the imbalanced and dire realities of the world that we have created and are currently choosing to go along with. Hopefully then, with a more complete picture of our predicament regarding where greed has been leading us, we can truly look at real long term resolutions and healing for this disease; for until humankind, as a race, can overcome their propensity towards selfish fear and greed, then nothing fundamental will really change for the better in our world.

A very good analogy, that has been used to illustrate the minuscule time of influence that humans have had on planet Earth, in relation to its total timeline of evolution, is to condense the 4.5 billion years of the entire evolution of the Earth down into just one year. If we start on January 1st of this year, then it is not until about November 15th that there are the conditions for an explosion of more complex and diverse forms of animal life, that begins to increase more rapidly. The dinosaur era begins around December 17th, before the mass extinction events around

December 26th wipes out around 75% of all species existing at that time. Carnivora mammals don't begin to appear until as late as December 28th, and primates, apes (our nearest genetic relatives) and gorillas, were living in their extended family social groups near the end of December 30th.

Around 8.20pm on the last day, homo erectus started to master fire in areas of Africa, Europe and Asia, and around 11.36pm, homo sapiens were sharing the Earth with other humanoids, such as Neanderthals and Denisovans. By 11.58pm on this final day of the year, the other humanoids have vanished, and the only remaining species, Homo sapiens, have begun to develop their rise and eventual dominance of the natural world. Modern humankind have only been around for the final few seconds in this analogy, and yet, in that time, they have come to multiply, explore and spread into every area of the planet. They have learned to design, utilise and build habitats, tools and technologies, way beyond any previous animal race. They have developed organised societies, education and communication systems, to continually build upon their progress and knowledge base, and they have even managed to begin to explore space and consider life beyond this planet. This humankind, with a long dark history of war and violence behind its progressions, has become so dominant, so quickly, that it has not yet fully understood its impact on the balance of the natural world that sustains its very existence, and this is the lesson and challenge that we are all now being faced with.

What caused this immense acceleration in Homo sapiens rise stills mystifies the scientific community (there are many theories, perhaps even the intervention of a more evolved, cosmic creative intelligence?), but what can't be denied, is that in our conscious development and ingenuity, we have come to affect the balance of our natural world in extremely profound and damaging ways; destabilising many of its integrated ecological cycles, that have been developing their intricate balance over billions of years. The main reason for this, due to its lack of foresight and intelligence, is the selfish imbalance caused in thinking and perception by the psychological disease of human Greed. This can lead to the human mind becoming both narcissistic and psychopathic, and where greed takes a hold of thinking, then taking, building, expanding, dominating and controlling, becomes a tunnelled and ignorant vision, that discards and even destroys any other forms of life that get in its way.

This is what I hope to clarify in the journey of the words ahead of you. I genuinely believe, that without some significant and collective change in our thinking and direction in the years ahead of us, then we are heading towards worldwide catastrophic societal collapse, mainly due to greed and the unsustainable forms of capitalist government and economics that it has established across the modern human world. We will need a genuine collective turning point, a collective realisation and awakening, a real step forwards in our own journey of evolution as a species, to overcome the hold that the disease of greed currently has over us.

At some point we will need to move away from the dominance of our old outdated animal programming of fear and self-preservation above all other life. We will have to move beyond the violent habits and psychological damages of our warring histories, and hopefully into a more collective state of being where we truly become a more universally intelligent race, that fully appreciates the natural sustainable cycles of all life on this planet. Once we truly realise that sustainability is the core foundation to survival, then we will naturally build all of our social structures around this reality, and we will fully invest in supporting all of our ecosystems, to enable both them, and us, to flourish. Who knows then what the rest of the universe may have to offer and teach us beyond such a step forwards, once we have learned to get our own house fully in order.

    I write with a combination of general research, simplified and summarised but with little of the tedium of endless accreditation and reference, and with a lifetime of personal study into human psychology and the human condition. While scholastic works are numerous on these subjects and our subsequent psychology, they often tend to alienate many readers by the complexities of their specialist terminologies and subject matters, and by the shear weight of their statistics and references. The aim of this book is certainly to simplify the ideas and processes of our mind's development through history, to write something that is hopefully engaging and easy to read and follow, and to give a clear picture of how greed has grown and developed within our cultures to come to create so many instabilities. Hopefully, everyone, regardless of age and background, will be able to read and understand the message here.

    While the fine detail of statistics and reference play a small part, they are mostly approximations and estimates that only serve to help to paint the bigger picture. And it is being able to see the bigger picture that is the real focus of this book, for this is what I believe, 'we all really need to know'; if only to aid in our ability to make more informed choices about the challenges now facing us all.

    Nothing ever written will be to everyones' tastes, but I write with one simple philosophy in mind, that I apply to all reading and information: read it, digest its meaning, but ultimately make up your own mind. If you don't have the time or desire to read the entire book, then please feel free to just skip to chapters 9, 10 and 11, for these offer the widest perspectives as to the bigger picture of our current global predicaments. I hope you all find at least something within the pages of this book, no matter how small, that educates and interests.

My positive thoughts and best wishes stand with you on the road ahead,

Jamie Best - 20th June 2024

Chapter 1: The Human Animal

So how has greed been allowed to become such a dominant and destructive influence within the psyche of human nature; where did it all begin and what is at the very root of the cause of this disease. Well there are two main factors as to how and why this disease has developed and become so prevalent within human nature. The first sits as the root cause to enabling greed to come into being in the first place, and stems from the innate animal instincts that still control and direct nearly all of humanity: the instincts toward self-survival and propagation, and their generation of the powerful primal emotion of fear. For all the intelligence and ingenuity that has developed within us as a species over the centuries, unfortunately, we are still mostly controlled by our base animal instincts, that have been so firmly imbedded within us over almost countless generational cycles of our evolution. These genetic animal instincts are like a written programming, playing again and again behind the scenes, throughout every type of experience and challenge we face. They simply will not change, until we can either override or rewrite and redirect the programming.

The second factor that has allowed the disease of greed to progress so deeply into the human psyche and on to controlling so many of our current systems of government and finance, relates to the expansion of the human mind and its ability to conceive time. This development has enabled us to individually make conscious decisions about how we choose to react to our animal instincts and fears, and to how we decide to express them and compensate for them in the world we build and control around ourselves. It has also enabled us to create and progress imagined fears and threats to our potential wellbeing, and to project these into the future, so that our thinking and behaviours might adjust and compensate, possibly even at the expense of other people and forms of life, to try to avoid having to face those imagined fears.

This second factor we will look to delve into and explore more later, as we look into how humanity's consciousness has expanded and how we began to organise and structure our societies more. So for now, in this first chapter, we will start at the beginning, with the very origin and root of all human greed, which lies in our ingrained animal nature and instincts, and in particular, the impulse of fear. Fear is where it all begins in the decision making processes; how we individually choose to react, and later more collectively, in the type of environment and world we then come to form and build around ourselves.

Animals, in fact all living organisms, seem to have an inbuilt set of protocols to their existence and propagation; a kind of programming, that I would endeavour to suggest comes from a very real creative intelligence, for without it, nothing in creation would continue to survive, develop or adapt. Now for animals, this can be divided up into three distinct principles, although they are all connected and part of the same protocol and reasoning: to continue existing. Ingrained within us all, at the the very core of our animal nature, there lies three main primal instincts and impulses: self-survival, reproduction, and adaptation. These are the primary instincts and directives of all evolving animals and organisms on this planet, and we, as humans, have never become separated from these impulses; we are all human animals.

Within the huge array of species that have populated this planet over the ages, there has been an amazing diversity of different types of processes and triggers that serve to activate these primal instincts and their senses and impulses. For the earliest humanoids, basic survival needs were really quite simple, but not without their various environmental challenges. As with most mammals, we were driven to be near regular sources of food and water, the two greatest essentials for life, or to know how to track and find these things, were either source to dry up or need variable options. Depending on the climate of where they were living, or perhaps if they were nomadic and wondered through different climatic areas, then some forms of animal skins or rudimentary clothing might be required to keep warm, especially if temperatures dropped lower at night. And finally, especially if there were known predators of humans in the area, or perhaps other rival human groups, then some type of shelter might be required, for both protection from possible attack and also from the elements.

If we had good sources of these basic elements for life, then life could become fairly stable, and the same still holds true for today, in our modern societies. One particular discovery and development of early humanoids, that hugely acted to separate and elevate us above the rest of the animal kingdoms, was the eventual mastery of fire. All animals naturally fear fire, as it is an immediate threat to their lives, if it gets out of control or cannot be escaped. Now somewhere around a million or so years ago (it is hard to pinpoint any exact dates or causes), early humanoids began to learn to control and eventually master fire. This afforded a number of benefits and opened up doors for us to explore and progress further in our evolution, and it also must of been quite a liberating and empowering discovery for early humans.

Being able to light and control fire was great for warmth, light and security, for warding off predators, and later on, humanoids realised that it could be used to cook meat and food, which was then more energising and easier to digest. We also later learnt that fire could be used to forge and shape tools and hunting weapons, and the mastery of fire meant that we could begin to explore into other regions, where colder, harsher climates may previously have been an issue. Mastering fire also gave us a real experience of conquering fear, as we would previously have feared the threat of fire and its uncontrollable nature. The benefits and liberation of conquering this fear would have been a big impetus in our meteoric rise as animals, and it may have created new motivations, in seeking to explore and face other fears, and previous unknowns in our natural world and its many diverse environments.

These though are the most basic elements of need that we are driven to seek and develop resources of, as human animals: food, water, warmth, shelter and safety. If any of the sources of these are threatened in any way, or indeed if we are threatened by predators or rivals, then fear may quickly kick in to stimulate a response to resolve the issues of the threat. This is how our nature's programming works to keep us alive and keep us evolving, and you can still see today that these needs are the foundations of survival in any modern day family unit and organised society: food, water, warmth, shelter and safety. If you have all of these, then life can seem very comfortable indeed, and if all of these are easily maintained, then the mind's focus certainly has more opportunity to learn and progress in other areas of questioning and development.

For this chapter though, we are looking to establish an understanding of our earliest and most deeply ingrained instincts and impulses. If our lives or our resources and our security were threatened in some way, then the impulse of fear would immediately kick in to motivate a reaction or response, simply to keep us alive and breeding. Fear is a very distinct primal emotion, and it sits behind and instigates a large proportion of our human behaviours, directed of course towards our ultimate survival and our propagation. Psychologically, our possible responses to feeling fear, are quite straight forward: at its most extreme, if we are faced with something that might kill us, we are forced to make an instant assessment and reaction: either we fight and hopefully destroy the threat, or we flee, to hopefully live to see another day. These are our instinctive responses to any threat and fear, to fight or flee. There is also the possibility of 'freezing' in indecision, but with natural selection and evolution there is evidence to suggest, that the animal that hesitates and freezes nearly always ends up dead, so there may not be so much evidence within the gene pool of the animals that choose to freeze.

The emotion of fear can have a very powerful effect on both our body and mind: in an instant the heart rate and breathing can rapidly increase, to circulate blood and prime our senses and physical agility, and the mind and senses can become super focused and alert, ready to direct the immediate action that could ultimately decide whether we live or die. Fear is a stimulant and type of excitement to the body and mind, and the hormone adrenaline is quickly released into the body to facilitate this rapid increase in blood flow, agility and primed senses. Our reaction to fear and its powerful body altering influences, can go one of two ways: either we react, in our quick assessment of fight or flight and move into action (we compensate the fear and face the threat in some way), or, we are overcome with the fear and fall apart and crumble (failing to act we become subdued or dominated by the threat and fear).

Again, complete subjugation by fear causing inaction is not a common outcome in nature, as this means the imposition of the threat is in control, which more often in nature means death to that which is under threat, when the ultimate aim of the programming is survival. But as we look deeper into the development of the psychology of fear through human evolution, then the choice of inaction and subjugation by fear opens up many new branches of behaviours, psychological imbalances and illnesses in humanity, which we may look at in later chapters. Something we will also look at in more depth, as it very much has been associated with the development and spread of greed, is how fear can be used to subdue and control others. For example, if you understand how fear works and how to induce fear, knowing it's possible programmed reactions, then you also have the potential to instigate and control behaviours that are directed by this programming, perhaps even en masse, on a collective scale.

Let us have a quick look at a few simple examples to illustrate the more immediate reactions to threats and the impulses of fear. As an early humanoid animal, living in a small social family group, we are making our way to a stream, as one of our known natural sources of water. We know other animals use this for water, some of which may be predatory, so we are already on alert in case we come across an immediate threat. As we approach the stream, a large animal that had been hidden behind foliage makes a charge at us: in an instant fear instigates adrenaline, which instigates an immediate decision and reaction: - the threat seems large and may be too strong to fight and overcome - so we run for our life. Knowing the area, looking for a safe respite or simply to outrun our pursuer, we decide instantly to flee and hopefully to live another day.

Another example could be the threat of a rival humanoid group along the boundaries of our normal environment: we might be hunting at the edge of our group's territory and have several of our group members with us, primed and ready to stalk and kill for food. We might then come across a single member of another rival humanoid group, who perhaps is lost or partially wounded. They might react ready to defend themselves out of fear, while we, feeling confident with the rush of fear and adrenaline, that we are stronger and have more numbers with us, may decide to fight and try and kill or drive off the rival. A different threat with a different reaction to fear, each based on a quick assessment under the impulses of fear and adrenaline, as to what might provide the best chances of survival. They are simple examples, but both illustrate how the fear programming works. The more successful the judgements we make in the moment under the influence of fear and adrenaline, then the more ingrained the behaviours become, and the more successful the social group may become at surviving and reproducing.

Most fear traces back to the threat and fear of suffering and death, it is intrinsically linked to our survival instinct; the fear of not having enough food or good shelter, ultimately, if not reacted to and compensated for, could then lead to our suffering and possible death. So improving these things, food and water sources, ways to hunt and gather food, warm practical clothing, safe and secure shelter; these all become motivating focal points in our evolution and development, that stem from the fear of the lack of these elements and our desire to survive and adapt to our environment. The better we become at securing all of these survival essentials, then the more control we have over our environments and its potential threats, and the less we have to directly face those fears potentially. Here, as we develop all of these factors and skills, lies the earliest foundations of our evolving organised societies.

But of course, our experience of fear, even as early humanoid animals, is not always so simple as to just be triggered by immediate threats of danger. As we and our capacity to consciously assess our life and survival needs has evolved and developed, so our capacity to imagine and expand our scope of potential threats and fears, has also widened and progressed. As we have developed more complex social practices and lives, and more complicated egos and personas, then the lists of potential threats to the wellbeing of these aspects of ourselves, whether real or imagined, has also expanded and diversified. What fear does to our bodies and minds, and our basic impulses and reactions regarding other less immediate threats and fears, still remains the same though. Regardless of the many complexities of the human mind and the numerous elements of fear that it can choose to perceive in life, with all of the many unknowns of the world outside of our control; even if the fear is completely imagined and unlikely we may still experience it as a very real threat, and so compensate our behaviours and actions accordingly.

      This is where greed has had its field within the human psyche, and this is where behaviours have adapted and evolved to become more and more extreme over time, in seeking more and more compensation, more and more power and control, to fears, real and imagined, that have taken a hold of our thinking and simply will not go away while we entertain them. Greed begins with our primal animal fear impulses and instincts, and so the only real resolution and healing to the psychological imbalance of greed lies at this very root: to get to the point where we are ready to give up and overcome our fear and its control of our thinking and behaviours, and, like mastering fire, perhaps this just might be another huge step forward and liberation in our current evolution as humans.

Chapter 2: The Pack Mentality

Having now set the foundations of where we all, as human animals, have evolved from, and where the survival impulses of fear that can lead to imbalances of greed, drive to motivate our evolution in improving the strength of our survival in all its basic areas of need; the next stage we will have a look at, is the development and expansion of our social groups. Now that humans had conquered fire and were able to establish stronger more stable practices for maintaining their basic daily survival needs: food, water, shelter etc…, so their minds were afforded the time to begin to branch out and focus and develop in a whole host of other avenues and directions: the gradual development of common sounds and symbols that could lead to common languages; the shaping and development of tools for building, food preparation and hunting and defence; the later development of building stronger more defendable shelters and encampments; and the developments of social order and of more individuality within the small social groups that early humanoids lived within.

Wherever we branched out and explored, by both trial and error and the application of the mind, we began to expand our range of learning and experience, and so to develop, utilise and improve our skills and knowledge base. As animals go, humanoids have a very long period of nurturing their young to independence, and this affords much time for the passing on of skills and knowledge to strengthen the generational progressions being made. With more stable survival practices, so more time was available for socialising, and the hearth of the fire was often a safe focal point for these early social groups to gather around, to share ideas, experiences and stories, and develop socially.

These early humanoid groups were mostly nomadic hunter gatherers, both killing animals to feed themselves and eating off the plants and vegetation, according to what they had learnt to be sustaining and nutritious. They passed down to each younger generation the ever expanding practical knowledge and experience of their hunting techniques and of all the plants and trees that could help to feed them through their seasons, to supply them with raw building materials and even to help them to heal if they were sick or injured. These small nomadic humanoid social groups were originally very similar to their nearest genetic relatives, the primates, and more specifically the great apes. They probably most commonly consisted of around 10-30 people, give or take a few, composed of a few extended family groups of all ages; there might be one alpha male or leader, or a small number of older dominant males, that would have proved themselves in strength and resourcing food for the group.

The group, usually made up of dominant males, nurturing and fertile females and children of varying sexes and ages, would then have an established social order, especially regarding privileges such as feeding and mating rites. While there could sometimes be competition and conflict within such social groups, if food were scarce or perhaps when a young male grew to become more dominant and challenging, the established social order would usually maintain relative peace within the group, and allow for gregarious and friendly social bonds to develop. This again gave more time to develop other skills and knowledge that could ultimately benefit the survival of the group, and stronger bonds made for better pack mentalities in hunting and in conflicts with predators or other groups, increasing the chances of success and survival.

Thinking and living as part of a group, as opposed to just surviving as an individual, while it had its internal dangers of conflict, offered far more benefits to the individuals who chose to accept the social order. If the group came under threat by predators or rival groups, then a larger number of individuals working and fighting together, offered a much greater chance of survival. Working together as part of a group meant that more elaborate plans and techniques could be used to hunt and trap pray, and also that larger prays could be targeted, that would provide so much more by ways of meat and raw materials. There would always be lots of eyes and ears primed ready for threats and danger, and the alarm could be quickly raised and spread throughout the group if a threat appeared, so they were all quickly ready to react and defend themselves and each other.

And so the group, or 'pack' mentality, is another primary foundation to early human existence, still strongly exposed in our thinking and behaviours today. It has set within us an acceptance of certain social orders, an instinct of when to dominate or to yield and submit, and of course, when to challenge, should the social order or dominant behaviour become weak or unbalanced. In primitive times, imbalances would be more blatant and easier to see: a stronger more dominant male might choose to take more food for itself for example, leaving little for those lower down the social order, who would then go into the fear mode of starvation. If such an imbalance persisted, then it would create disharmony within the group, which could then lead to conflict and possibly even violence and death.

Ultimately, the whole group would suffer through the stresses of internal conflict, as disharmony and conflict breaks the established social order and bonds, and it simply wastes time and energy that could be better directed towards hunting and gathering, and the general prosperity of the group. Groups can become broken apart through conflict, with individuals forced to take sides, perhaps to the extreme where one side will exile or even obliterate the individuals on the other side, to reassert their dominance. Or, the group dynamics may shift to a harsher form of subjugation, where the stronger dominate and abuse the weak. Just take a look through the progressive pages of human history, and you will see the same primitive patterns, playing out again and again and again.

As stated earlier though, and proved by the fact that apes and then humanoid groups both evolved to continue to live in wider groups of social order and structure, there are far more benefits to the pack mentality and group living than there are disadvantages. While you might have to be subservient to the stronger more dominant individuals, and go along with the general consensus of thinking and leadership decisions, if you were not particularly strong or skilled in hunting, you would have a much greater chance of obtaining food and surviving within an organised group. You could learn and develop more skills within a group, have more chance of mating and passing on your gene pool, and working as part of a group, you might be able to build stronger, more durable and safer shelters, that were less likely to come under threat.

The group mentality, whilst offering more physical security in numbers and greater chance of an individual's survival, also started to help the human mind to expand and develop more collectively. As humans developed common signs, symbols and early languages, as ways to direct hunting techniques perhaps or to pass on knowledge, regarding the implementation of tools and building or cooking techniques for example, then the more we began to establish common frames of reference and of thinking.

Our minds began to recognise and share these common frames of reference, from which we could then begin to form sounds and symbols, that could communicate a common understanding and perhaps even start to relate ideas. It was the start of a more collective mind and way of thinking and communicating.

While with increased social time, that allowed for the start of rudimentary developments in art, clothes and jewellery making, and for greater individuality in how we began to represent ourselves; living within a larger social group, also meant that we could start to think more collectively, regarding how our group was to progress and prosper, and the type of skills that we all shared and could excel in. The individual survival instincts, that could instigate fear and our need to adapt and protect, might now begin to expand and encompass our collective group more, as we might start to consider and think of this as a genuine extension of our individual self; the beginning perhaps, of our gradual coming together and evolution as one worldwide human race.

For many thousands of years humans developed and evolved within these more nomadic social groups, gradually improving their tool making and building skills, improving their forms of communication with each other and expanding their in-depth knowledge of the natural world that they depended upon for survival. Social groups began to become more distinct, with many individual tribes starting to develop a rudimentary shamanic relationship with nature, and a veneration for their ancestral heritage and knowledge. Some of these tribes would often seasonally move between, and temporarily settle in their more favoured areas, depending where food and water sources were more readily available. Due to this their camp sites and shelters started to become more established and elaborate, and as well as individual family shelters, so larger communal buildings started to be constructed and to be used socially and ceremoniously.

These were the beginnings of our language and cultural developments, with many thousands of years of tribal history behind them. With the mastery of fire and the developments of clothes and tool making, some nomadic tribes would become more explorative, and gradually through time, more tribes would come into contact with each other and venture to develop some common communication, allowing for the possible trade of tools and knowledge, and of course, in some cases, to interbreed more and spread their gene pool. This social networking all started to happen more around some 130,000 years ago (as an anthropological estimate from dated remains), and within large regions where higher populations could be supported, there gradually grew many networks of interacting small social tribes.

It certainly wasn't just a simple case of everyone just getting along and sharing with each other though, far from it in fact. The first meetings of tribes could be a very tense and fearful event, with the possible danger of violence, fighting and death, were anything to tip the tensions over the edge. Posturing, strength and pride would all be on display via the tribal leaders and hunters, to show that they were not to be messed with and must be respected. Gifts and coupling between eligible sexes of the tribes were good ways to cement the bonds and agreements between them, and greater numbers of allies could also mean greater strength and security, and a sense of greater people power.

The other side of more social groups and tribes coming into contact however, started to develop a whole other faction and psychology in early humanoids: that of the warriors and war makers. And this mode of fearful and aggressive thinking has had a strong influence on human development and our expansions across the globe, still influencing and causing conflict in our modern day world today, where the size of armies and tools of war can now be hugely destructive. It has also helped to feed and inflate the psychological imbalances of greed, for if you start to see other social groups as merely a threat with whom you have to share resources, then perhaps by eliminating this threat and any others you come across, you might continually be able to increase the resources you have at your disposal and control. In fact, such thinking could start to become insatiable if followed, as with each victory you could feel more powerful and dominant, and your resources become ever more abundant. The initial natural impulses are just basic fear and survival, but the progressed expressions of these, taken to their extremes, can then become a psychology of war, pillaging and destruction, that leaves little or no respect for other forms of life.

In our early tribal existence as humanoids, some tribes chose to focus on war with other tribes, and to develop a fierce nature and reputation. This was one possible way to improve your survival chances, should you develop greater strength and better weapons and fighting techniques; taking the resources of others could be easier sometimes than having to hunt and gather your own. So one possible avenue for human social development, was to embrace fear and to use this to impose dominance on others, and as this mode of thinking started to evolve, so it then began to look to any means necessary to achieve its aims, and ultimately, to gain more control of the resources that are essential for life and survival.

Tribal histories of war and conflict, and deep set enmities, began to develop in certain regions and areas where peoples were in competition and conflict for resources and control, and later, as social groups and tribes expanded and settled in larger populations, so many of these long held tensions and conflicts transferred into larger wars between neighbouring nations and peoples. Nations that invested in armies and the psychology of war, then began to look farther afield at how they could expand and conquer other lands and peoples, and it was often down to their leader's drive, greed and ambition, as to how far they went and how much they conquered.

The other side of the gains of victory over others and the increased control of resources, is then revealed in the reverse psychological fear of loss: if you think in terms of attacking and taking from others, then the mind is more susceptible to the fear that others may seek to do the same to you, and so behaviours of fear, in attack and defence, can grow and expand and begin to dominate the mind more. Also, the more that you have amassed and taken from others, then the more you may fear to lose, and in this mode of thinking, the imbalances of fear and greed can really take a hold of the mind and its subsequent reactions.

Chapter 3: The Alpha Male, Leadership and Domination

So it has probably become clear by now that I am not looking to go into any great depth regarding the anthropological history of humankind. In our scholastic developments and scientific research over many centuries and generations, we have amassed a real wealth of informed knowledge, proven science and philosophy regarding human evolution. I am attempting to use some of this, in a simple way, to help to focus on and outline the real topic of this book: greed, and the growth of its psychological hold on the mind and behaviours of humanity, as we have continued to evolve and multiply as a species. Through the building blocks of each chapter, we can then begin to develop a clearer picture of how we got to our present predicament and reality, where greed has been enabled to cause so much destruction and imbalance within our world.

At the very root of greed, through all of its many guises and proponents, there is just simple primitive animal programming and fear, nothing of any great intelligence. From these beginnings of fear, through our tribal developments, some humanoids and groups chose to embrace and listen to their fears more than others; to begin to view other groups more as competition and threats, as oppose to potential allies. Subsequently, from following such thinking, so the psychology of making war began to develop more within the human psyche. With tribes seeking to make war with other tribes, as an actual means to hunt and gather, and to gain more resources and control over areas of land, then it became more of a necessity for all tribes to become practiced in the art of combat. Even if you weren't a tribe that had chosen to seek out and attack others for their resources, to be able to defend your tribe against such aggressions, you would need to become fierce enough to meet fire with fire, to be able to survive such an attack.

Another part of the developing nature of some primate groups, and transferred across to early humanoid social groups and their social orders, was the innate male impulses of what has been termed the 'alpha male' instinct. While not all groups would have just one dominant alpha male, and larger groups might rely upon several of the strongest dominant males for leadership, the alpha male sat at the very top of the social order. While there could also be a social hierarchy amongst the females, headed by an alpha female, nearly all primate and early humanoid groups were male dominated and lead by what has become known as, the alpha males.

The original development of the role of alpha male evolved from the base instinctive impulses we mentioned within the first chapter. It is a role to promote survival: survival of the fittest and strongest gene pool, but also of the more intelligent leadership in decision making, regarding the welfare of a social group. Throughout the animal kingdoms and especially relatable amongst mammals, their is a whole host of male dominated displays and competitions that have evolved, sometimes leading to direct conflict and battle between challenging dominant males, all to win the title of 'alpha' and to secure feeding privileges and mating rites with the females. This is, of course, just nature's way of insuring that the strongest and fittest genes get passed on and built upon within each particular species, but it is also establishing the behaviours that the strongest, most dominant or violent male, has more chance to survive and prosper, and even to control and direct its own particular social group.

The role and position of alpha male within its social group, is an enviable one amongst the competing males, and perhaps for all the members of the group, from each of their differing perspectives. The males aspire to it and instinctively aim to prepare and grow stronger into adolescence, to eventually reach the impulses to assert their own dominance, and to achieve a ranking in the social order as high as possible, perhaps even as alpha. But becoming alpha is certainly not an easy and stress free path, for while it offers many rights and privileges, it also comes with a whole host of responsibilities, challenges and potential threats. As the role of alpha male, or leader, continued to evolve and develop within early humanoid groups, then there grew a whole host of both positive and negative expressions and representations of the role, that leaders were usually free to make their own individual choices about, as few would ever question their decision making or authority, knowing the possible consequences of conflict with a powerful dominant male.

The privileges of winning the status of alpha male were many. By sheer size and dominance and by proving your strength in any challenges or conflict, you might begin to feel an inflated sense of yourself and your importance within the group. When food was hunted or gathered, then you would have first pickings and be able to take the best bits for yourself, and you could also oversee the order of pickings for others in your group; enabling you, if you were wise, to strengthen certain bonds and allegiances that could further support the security of your status.

The alpha male, once established within the group, would then receive respect and perhaps special favours from others within the group. Social bonds, and sometimes even gifts would automatically come to and favour the alpha, to stay on his good side and show reverence and allegiance, for the better placed you are beside the alpha male, then the higher up the social order you might climb, and the more privilege you might receive yourself. The alpha male would have a primary choice of the best resting spots in their encampments, and they might be afforded more elaborate shelters, were the group to stay in favoured areas for any length of time.

One of the top privileges, was of course winning the rights to mate with perhaps a number of the most physically (genetically) 'attractive' females. The alpha male got to pass on the strength of his genes, and become patriarchal father to the group, as well as the genetic father of many of the next generation, if he were lucky. Although mating was heavily dominated by the alpha male within many primate groups, within early humanoid groups, there may have been more numbers, variety and diversity, and more mating between pairs of male and females; needless to say though, being the strongest and a leader, would afford more receptive females, and some tribal communities had leaders who mated with many women and fathered many children. It is another genetic foundation passed on through primates to early humanoids, to maintain and reproduce the fittest and strongest gene pool possible, to offer the greatest chances of survival, adaptation and prosperity.

So alpha males could live like and experience privilege like kings, indeed there are many parallels with how the realities of leaders, kings and emperors of our later societies, originated from the early humanoid thinking and behaviours towards an alpha male. There is another long trail of gradual evolution and development here, from the primitive and often brutish origins of leadership won by domination and threats of violence, to the later positions of elaborate privilege and control of kings, and the subservience of the many individuals who made up the particular tribe or nation. As human societies expanded and progressed across the globe, so different cultures raised up and dressed their leaders in different titles and robes, often affording them god-like rule over their lands and subjects. Gradually their roles became more the inheritance of their bloodlines, and their shows of strength and impositions of fear, turned more to their cunning and intelligence in rulership, and more importantly, with ultimate power over their subjects, to their balance of cruelty and mercy and the might and numbers of their obedient armies.

As stated earlier though, being alpha male, or leader, did not just come with an endless abundance of positive privileges and easily maintained power and dominance. The role of leader within a primitive social group, and later within larger human societies, always carried with it large potential threats and stresses, and huge responsibilities, regarding the survival and wellbeing of the whole group. In earlier social groups nearly all the decisions fell upon the alpha: if the group was nomadic and became short of sources of food for example, then it was up to the alpha to find alternative sources, or to decide when and where to move to find fresh resources. The whole group could live or die on such decisions.

If the group came under threat from predators or rival groups, then it was up to the alpha to step up and utilise his fierce strength. He would have to decide their fight or flight response to best protect them, and he would have to inspire and lead his warriors in conflict, were it necessary to stand and fight. Then there was also the possibility of a threat to the alpha male position coming from within the social group. If the alpha was not unanimously liked or considered wise enough to make good decisions, or if a younger strong male wished to rise up the ranks, then the threat of rebellion and challenge to the alpha male might always be just around the corner. Sometimes the leaders of other regional groups might also wish to challenge and dethrone the alpha male, to steal his resources and women, and sometimes even to destroy his entire genetic line.

So a good and successful leader always had to be aware and possibly ahead of such threats, to maintain social order and his position as alpha; he had to start to think more about maintaining and utilising his role and the power it afforded. As humanity continued to develop consciously and started to be able to project their thoughts and hopes and desires more into the future they envisioned, then the ability to plan and to act upon these desires became a stronger influence on actions and behaviours. For leaders of social groups and then larger organised societies, this meant, with the power and control they had over their subservient followers, that they could develop ambitions for more power and control, and to begin to utilise their followers as possible armies for gaining more resources and lands.

This is where the separation becomes more apparent in human psychology, between the positive and negative expressions and developments of alpha male dominance and leadership. A 'good' leader might be seen to be fair to all the members of his social group, and wise in his decision making, regarding their survival. He might ensure that food is shared out more fairly through the social order, and he might spend more time on developing positive social bonds with the group. A good leader, and obviously I use the word good as relative to the fairness given to the group as a whole, would learn that the stronger the positive social bonds are within a group, and the better fed and happier they are, then the more they might unite and work and stand together for the betterment of all individuals. This is certainly a thinking and approach to leadership that can yield success and create greater harmony within its social orders.

But human individuals think and react in different ways, and another approach to leadership and the power it afforded, perhaps not viewed to be so good by all the members of the group, was to rule more by domination, subjugation and fear. Following this line of thinking could lead to the development of leaders who might become more merciless dictators: leaders who took more for themselves and did not care so much for those at the lower ends of their social order, leaders who might become ambitious for more power, lands and resources, and leaders who might see war and the expansion of armies as the strongest way forward to ensure survival and continuation of their blood lines. Leaders of such fearful aggression would have more fearing, subservient followers, and where the individual's mind is restricted from thinking for itself more, so it remains weak in that respect, and can so much more easily be dictated to and directed, according to the ambitions of its leader.

Unfortunately, the more aggressive and ambitious leaders often forcefully gained more followers and built stronger armies, and so historically they had more success in invading and colonising lands. This allowed for the evolution of more of the psychology of greed and domination to become established within our social orders over the centuries, which, in turn, has enabled this thinking of greed to learn to master control of both governments and economies, where the power and resources all lie; even if the means to this control has had to become more hidden from the general populations over time. Leaders of early humanoid groups, with real desires and ambitions to expand their territories and their control and dominance of resources and followers, were then the first real advocates of greed in human society; enabling it to start to take a hold of the mind's of individuals in positions of power, and advertising its thinking and behaviours to all within their social group as a means to success, that should be looked up to, admired and emulated.

These are the two basic directions that can be followed in the developing psychology of human leadership. As they have developed over many centuries and generations, they have branched and diversified and come to be personified within the names of our historic leaders of migrations, colonisations and nations. These we will look at in more depth in later chapters. For now, however, we look to mark the distinction between the different possible approaches to leadership that have developed from the alpha male psychology, and in particular, the ambitions towards greater power and control, for this is what can lead to the growth of the imbalance of greed, and the resulting destructive ignorance to other life that it can enable.

Within these two basic approaches to leadership, there is also the beginnings of two very important archetypes in human nature and psychology. The just and fair minded, caring leader who may still have to fight to protect his people, is depicted as the heroic and inspirational archetype; perhaps embodying all that is deemed 'good' in human nature. While the ambitious and merciless leader desperate for wealth and power, who seeks to dominate and kill the peoples of other societies, is depicted more as the despot and evil archetype; embodying the qualities that are deemed as 'bad' in human nature. These archetypes and their conflicting ethics are prevalent everywhere, in many different cultural forms, throughout the developing human societies spread out across the globe. They represent a deeper ongoing internal battle within humanity, with our developing morality and ethics to life, and the wars and battles between them have been raging throughout our entire recorded history to date.

So, the establishment of the alpha male thinking, leadership and domination, are all there as part of our developing human psychology. To briefly go back over the premise of this particular chapter, to help to clarify this stage of our human development that leads on from our animal genetics and sets our base impulses as humans; while singular alpha males may not be common across the entire spectrum of the animal kingdoms and its numerous species, they are prevalent in the primates closest to our genetic evolution. While some primate groups do not have dominant alpha males who always lead, and some have similar size males and females who both have their own hierarchical structures; the thinking and behaviours of male dominance and aggression, to dominate others within their social group and to seek to control essential resources and to have more food and the pickings of the best, are very real and established primitive instincts. They are part of our primitive psychology as humans, and they have continued to evolve within human societies right up to our present day.

And so the principles and psychology of seeking privilege and control through endeavouring to win alpha male status, has become established and developed within humanoid thinking and behaviours. It has, over time, branched out into a whole host of other behaviours and thinking, of ways to secure more rights, more resources and more selfish control of the social orders; all primarily to increase one's own chances of survival and prosperity. The more this thinking is invested in, then the more potentially it can take over and become obsessive, narcissistic, psychopathic even. And when thoughts turn only to one's own well being and prosperity and how much resources can be controlled and acquired for one's own survival above all other life, then the psychological imbalance of greed can take over, starting to dictate all thinking, actions and behaviours.

Such greed becomes a disease, taking over an individual's mind and thinking, but also potentially seeking to project itself out into the social order, to justify itself and to create and establish positions of power and control. True dominance and might in early humanoid groups came from physical strength and combat skill, but it required others within the social group to become subservient; an alpha male becomes more powerful, according to the numbers of his loyal followers. The alpha male usually ruled by the threat and imposition of fear and violence; were his strength or leadership rights to be questioned or challenged, then you could meet a painful and violent end. While other more positive attributes of leadership were also important to a successful and growing social order, such as wise decision making for the groups wellbeing, and fairness in the sharing of food for example, the deciding factor in most challenges was more often male brute force and strength. This is what then sets the base tone for nearly all developing patriarchal human societies, and if power and greed began to affect the thinking of those within the privileged alpha positions of leadership, then the populations under their rule would prosper or suffer according.

Chapter 4: The Growth of Early Human Societies

In this next chapter, we will start to look at how the earliest human social groups gradually progressed from ape like extended family groups, on towards more organised tribes and societies made up of more numerous family groups, and, eventually, into establishing larger structured towns, cities, regions and nations. Current science favours that the first humanoid hunter gatherer groups started to appear in Africa several million years ago. Africa is a large continent with many and varied climates and eco-systems, that in turn offered many different types of environments from which to hunt and gather food and resources. If the lands held plenty of water and were lush in vegetation, then they might support and offer many different animal food sources and many regularly available types of edible plants, fruits, nuts and berries. Whereas if the climate was hotter and the land drier, then food sources might be less easily available.

Climate and environment, were the major contributing factors to the numbers of human individuals that could be supported to survive within these early social groups. If the lands were fruitful and water sources readily available, then larger family groups could flourish within an expanding tribe, and the tribe may not have to move around so much for its food and water, enabling shelters or encampments to become more developed and organised. On the other hand, if vegetation was sparse and water harder to find, then animal populations and plant food sources would be less readily available, so human groups might be restricted to smaller numbers that could be supported by the harsher environment, and that could move about more freely to find sustenance. The need to find more abundant environments for supporting life was probably one of the primary factors that contributed to human's increased explorations and migrations across the globe, eventually to come to live and exist in every type of climate group. But for this to happen, then a whole host of other survival skills had to be discovered, learnt and developed.

Other variable factors would also dictate the comfortable numbers of individuals that could be maintained within these early social groups. The types and numbers of predators that might exist within naturally abundant areas, where water and food sources were more abundant, would also have an effect, due to increased threats and competition for resources. More abundant environments might also mean that more rival human groups could exist within a more confined area, which again could increase potential threats, conflict and competition. If there was increased conflict between tribes over hunting areas and resources, then usually the stronger more fearsome tribes would prevail, thus serving to reinforce the genetic progression of these attributes in humans.

Different environments and climates would pose different types of problems and sometimes challenges unique to the particular area. For groups that were native to these different areas, then different specific types of tools and weapons were gradually developed, with different skills and techniques in hunting and different knowledge bases to the fauna and flora. All of these elements would add to the distinction of each tribe, and the types of cultures and beliefs that might gradually develop over the centuries. Even today there are living remnants of hunter gatherer tribes still in existence in our world, and their depth of knowledge to their environments and skills in finding food and water, is often quite unique and truly amazing to behold. But the type of skills that would be needed to venture into more unknown environments and other varying climates, would include things that would have to be learned and developed more along the way.

From the initial spread and establishment of human groups across Africa, there then came the migrations into Eurasia and Indonesia and eventually into the rest of the world. Early groups lived mostly in caves and natural shelters, but as they explored more diverse environments, then the need to be able to construct safe and practical shelters grew. Shelters around the protection of the hearth of the fire became more popular, to keep warm and to ward off predators, so building shelters that could adapt to this need also developed and evolved. Mastering fire, and then being able to transport or set fires in environments that could be cold or wet, was a vitally important skill for survival in general, and then, even more so, for explorations into new unknown territories. But there were also many other skills that became focuses of development and culture as we migrated and settled in other lands.

Skills in cooking, food preparation and food preservation, all become important focuses of development as we ventured to explore new environments. If you were starting to explore new areas where you could not be certain of the types of food that might be available, then the more food that you could preserve and take with you, the more time you might have to establish new hunting and gathering routines. Cooked food it seems, may not have really begun to develop until much further down the line of our evolution, as we learned that it was warming and took less energy to digest, and in time, we also learned that smoking meats could help to preserve them for long periods. But preparing and preserving foraged nuts and fruits that could be carried with you as you travelled, could offer a reliable energy source and mean that less time would be needed to hunt and gather whilst on the move.

Another vital set of skills that was in continual development, was the use of animal skins, bones and natural fibres to produce both clothing and carrying aids, for weapons, arrows, darts, food, tools and utensils. Larger animal skins or skins bound together, and also larger leaves and fibres could be used for protection from the elements in the advancing construction of shelters, that would all help to make life more comfortable and prosperous. As new lands were explored, then new species of both plants and animals were discovered, and new raw materials for the development of these skills became available, allowing humankind to adapt more, think and create more, and to really hone their skills over time in all the focuses of their societies survival needs and social developments.

The psychology of exploring new lands also offered humans plenty of scope for expansion and branching out into new lines of thought and development. Firstly it was another huge step forwards in the conquering of fear, for the many fears and threats of the unknowns of new, unexplored environments, would have felt very real and possibly daunting: what climates would they be able to survive? What new types of predators might they encounter? Would there be other fearsome tribes already established there? And would there simply be enough food and water to sustain their tribe? In light of all these possible fears and horrors, humankind still decided to face up to these and move forward and explore new environments; they faced up to the darkness of the unknown and progressed. This could only help to support the instincts of expansion and adventure more in our collective psychology, with the endorphins of success that could then sometimes follow, as new more provident lands were discovered, and tribes were enabled to expand and thrive.

The other challenges that enabled our expansion of the mind into the thinking of improved problem solving and the development of tools and living skills, were the many and varied diversities that new lands introduced and that had to be adapted to: different climates and different cycles of the seasons in northern and southern hemispheres, that offered different times of available foods and raw materials; different periods of day and night that could vary seasonally, and different climates of altitudes, that could present wholly unique eco-systems; different geographical locations that could offer more protective shelters and settlements, or more consistent sources of food, as with say coastal locations, where sea foods and fish might be abundant. All of these differences first challenged our minds in the problems they might have presented, which, in our need to quickly adapt and survive, stimulated our problem solving brains and continually strengthened these neural networks, through trial, error and success.

Over centuries of these explorations and psychological developments, life for many human social groups gradually expanded and improved. In the most abundant areas, life may have become less about the harsh battles just to survive and more about building up the strengths of each tribal culture, to start to enable humans to thrive within their environments. Populations within many tribes may have begun to sustainably increase slightly, as did the numbers of groups across the globe, while humans had continued to migrate into new lands and regions. But populations were still very much restricted by the natural resources that were available within their regions to hunt and gather, and that could naturally sustain their numbers comfortably. If populations rose too high then food might be over hunted and become more scarce, and people might suffer and starve, or have to find new areas that could provide for them.

Humans who spent their whole lives living within nature, and who had evolved within certain eco-systems over many thousands of years, gradually gained more of an insight to the balance and providence of the nature around them. Many of them started to develop a reverence for nature and the animals and plants that enabled their survival; some even began to form early religious or shamanic beliefs and rituals that expressed their respect, and possibly began to offer them more insight into, even communication with, the balance and spirit of their environments and eco-systems. This reverence for nature began another branch of our psychological development and exploration of the mind, for now humankind began to ponder where we had come from, what was behind our life and natural existence, and how we could try to interact with this all in some way.

If tribal life in some regions did begin to become more comfortable over time, and a more harmonic balance with nature was naturally maintained, there was still of course the other side of human nature and its desire to conquer, that was continuing to develop and had to be contended with for survival. More established communities may have allowed for more leisure time, which gave rise to the skills of leisure, in art, jewellery and totem making, and in ceremonial practices. Tribes that wanted to maintain the comforts of their relative harmony, would have learned that positive bonds and relationships with other tribes could help maintain their peace and prosperity. Trading tools and knowledge and perhaps crafted gifts, as well as allowing breeding between peoples of different tribes, all helped to enhance social bonds and regional stability.

What couldn't so easily be accounted for and bargained with, however, were the tribes and colonisers who had chosen fear and aggression as their primary survival weapons. Although there is not much archaeological evidence in history for early warring human groups, as so little is currently known about early humanoids, within the primate world of our closest relatives, the chimpanzees, these behaviours of intergroup aggressions and the brutal killing of neighbouring groups, have been more recently studied and witnessed. It has been proved through observation that chimpanzees do this in order to expand their groups and territories, and to enjoy the extra resources that this can yield. The human desire to kill and to take from and gain from the demise of other humans, has always been there, as a part of the brutality of nature and its primary impulse to survive. While the psychology of cooperation worked for some peoples in improving the stability of their survival chances, the fierce psychology of dominating and killing others to increase resources and chances of survival, was embodied and taken on by many other groups. These two opposing developing psychologies, of cooperation or subjugation, are at the heart of nearly all human conflict throughout our history and right up to the present day.

It is not until later in our recorded histories of human development, that we really begin to see these types of behaviour on a much grander scale, in migratory campaigns, wars, empire building and mass colonisations. But these potential instincts have always been an option within our primitive origins, and have certainly then come to play a major part in the shaping of our human world and its societies and nations. The same primitive instincts are at play offering the same sorts of rewards, of lands, resources and more potential mates and people power, only as time and human weaponry has progressed, the destruction and number of casualties has vastly increased. Human ambition and greed has been allowed to spread like a cancer throughout our developing nations and their very real, progressively more hidden, underlying principles of government and social control of populations.

This historical spread of domination and greed, following on from the migrations of the smaller, nomadic human social groups across the globe, did not begin to gain real momentum until the introduction of a practice and knowledge that changed completely the way humans lived in societies and groups, and which would explode their capacity to multiply and to settle permanently in larger designated territories. The practice that enabled and progressed this expansion of populations and social groups, was the utilising of farming and agriculture. This knowledge and set of skills finally enabled us to control our resources of food production, and to rapidly expand this to produce ever increasing numbers of crops and livestock.

The development and utilisation of agriculture could now enable more harmonious and stable societies to grow and exist. But, this would also be an enablement for larger and larger armies of warriors to be built up and trained in warfare, and, if the ambitions of some leaders within their cultures became directed towards territorial expansion, colonisations and empire building, they now had the means to develop and feed the armies that could help to achieve and realise such ambitions.

Chapter 5: The Historical Spread of Greed Through War, Imperialism and Colonisations

While the psychology of greed had already begun to develop within the human mind and its early societies, through the instincts to attack and take the territories and resources of others, the historical spread of greed really began to grow and gain momentum through larger human societies, as our populations rose in numbers and our leaders were held aloft more as all powerful monarchs and emperors. The desire for more wealth and power, the desire to steal and claim the lands and resources of other groups and tribes, and the desire to dominate and rule over peoples all began to start to dominate the thinking of many of our historic leaders. These were the two major factors that pushed the spread and development of greed within the human experience, and that really began to establish it as an extreme and potentially highly destructive disease of the mind: ambitious minded conquering leaders with almost omnipotent power, and growing subservient populations with trained and well equipped armies.

Thankfully, or maybe that is a strange way to describe viewing such a history, we have a long documented and recorded history of how the atrocities of war, aggressions, colonisations and the building of the concept of empires dominated so much of our historic growth and developments through this time. But having such records, if we are able to look at them more as detached observers rather than victorious products of such a history, does afford the ability to see the true nature of greed, for exactly what it is and the acts it can drive us to. While we were evolving and progressing in many positive ways through history: developing better societies; better farming and agriculture; better architecture and sanitation; better tools and inventions; better health knowledge and healing practices; better forms of art and philosophy…, these were all taking place alongside a continuing repetition of dominant wars, aggressions and invasions between growing populations and their nations.

A lot of the earliest known wars were centred around the cultures of Egypt, Nubia, Mesopotamia, Elam, Libya, Assyria, Babylonia, Canaan, the Hittites, to name just a handful, as there are literally hundreds of recorded conflicts between developing cultures in the 3000 years BCE, centred around the areas of the largest more established cultures. For the periods of between 3000-1000 BCE, then most of these conflicts were fought in the regions of Africa and the Middle East, where larger cultures had grown and developed around provident geographical locations. But there were also many historic and dynastic wars taking place through the regions of China and some in other areas of Asia, like India (the Kurushetra war 1050BCE for example) where wars over territory and rulerships became more regular. It was only in the next 1000 years BCE and beyond that larger wars took place more across the Mediterranean and Europe (while they still continued to be waged in the original areas of Africa, the Middle East and Asia), and then spread to other parts of the world, through the exploits of mass campaigns of colonisations and empire expansions.

Some of the major Mediterranean warring cultures included the Greeks, Romans, Spartans, Sicilians, Phoenicians, with numerous wars of conquest and empire building constantly being waged by the Assyrian Empire, Judah, Colchis, Babylonia, the Persian Empire, the Parthian Empire, the many Greek factions, the Roman Empire (and republic), and the many on-going dynastic wars and conflicts that continued throughout China. Again, this is all to name but a few of the cultures involved; humankind, and the cultures they were building through these times, were almost constantly at war with each other, mostly over land territories and their resources, following on from historic tribal disputes and developed enmities, but also mostly inspired and directed by ambitious and power hungry leaders: kings, emperors, war lords and despots. All of these were seeking to expand their kingdoms and proclaim the might of their particular culture and beliefs, all looking to write their names within history as some form of immortality for their egos, and all looking to increase the wealth and resources of their cultures through the spoils of war. This was all the perfect breeding ground for the spread of the disease of greed in human thinking and motivations, and to enable it to be held aloft and championed by these heads of state, for all humankind to look up to.

We then move across the dateline change over and into the next 1000 years CE, then the wars and campaigns begin to move up more into central and then Northern Europe. The Roman Empire continued its many campaigns and huge conquests, and the Chinese dynasties their on-going battles for states and empirical powers. There was also the rise of Islam during this time, and many Muslim military conquests that helped to spread their culture between Spain in the West and India in the East. The wars are truly relentless, spreading out from North Africa and the Middle East, throughout the Mediterranean, up into all areas of Europe and Asia, and back across from East Asia. So warring cultures would rise and fall, and new cultures would build up their armies and come into play: Armenians, Croatians, Hungarians, Germans, Franks, Gauls, Vikings, Celts; all had their times of war, and the list is extremely extensive.

Leading on to the our more recent history, past the period from the Middle Ages and into 1000 CE and beyond, right up until our present day, and the wars, campaigns and colonisations continued to progress. Wars would continue to spread and rage across all continents, backed and instigated by cultures, religions and beliefs of all kinds and races. The next passage of this chapter offers a brief run through of the major imperial movements and colonisations of the last millennium; responsible for numerous wars and atrocities, and for millions of murders and deaths. The numbers are truly astounding when you start to add them all up, and, if you add in all the previous millennia we have just mentioned, then there were hundreds of millions dying across this span of our history, due to the harsh direct realities and gore of battle and the subsequent after affects of war and military domination.

    The spread of the Islamic Caliphates rule and empire, and of the Roman and Byzantine Empire, both continued over many centuries and well into the early stages of this last millennium. During these times came the rise and spread of the Mongol Empire, to eventually become the largest contiguous land Empire in all history, until it started to fragment, divide and suffer under frequent rebellions. Then came the Ottoman Empire, originating in Turkey and spreading its control over more than 600 years across large areas of Europe, Asia and Africa. Later came the Mughal Empire, located in South Asia, noted for its architecture and cultural developments, but also well practiced in the arts of war to enable its expansion and control of this region; it was said to have tolerated and integrated the cultures it conquered more, instead of just subjugating and imposing its own structured rule. But war was nearly always the primary means by which all of these cultures expanded their territories and rulerships.

    Leaders generally became more secured and successful in their ruling positions for a time, amongst the chaos of these warring millennia, according to how much they could unify their people and build and train their armies. For this, they would obviously need lots of resources and wealth, good maintainable food supplies from agricultural systems that could be expanded with increased populations, and ever improving skills of combat and weapons development. Time, money and creativity would be poured into these endeavours; the tactics and 'art' of war would be developed and studied by the rulers and leaders of armies. Nations would often look to demonise their enemies, to unite and motivate their peoples and armies, and to make it easy to direct them into war. War was so popularised, that some nations even developed mercenaries; warriors and armies renowned for their fierceness and combat skills, willing to be hired and payed to fight and attack the enemies of their employers.

As this warring millennium progressed, around the time of the 15th and 16th centuries there began several European imperial expansions and colonial campaigns. These were the result of a combination of competitive and ambitious sovereign leaderships, powerfully constructed armies and navies, and, in part, the religious pilgrimages / inquisitions of the rising factions of Christianity, that had become more involved in controlling wealth, rulerships and their subjects. The Portuguese, Spanish, French, Dutch and English (later British), all began to make bold strides to expand their empires and seek more wealth and power for themselves. When they weren't caught up in fighting each other, these European colonisers were setting sail across the globe in search of new or 'unclaimed' lands, in the hope of claiming them for their king and country. These campaigns regularly became a competitive conflict and race, regardless of the rights of any previously established and native cultures within these new lands. Native peoples were often either converted to serve their new rulers and their imported religions, or they were decimated, with both of these outcomes, servitude and genocide, taking place in large numbers.

Firstly there began the Spanish Empire's expansions around the 15th century. Soon after the unification of Spain, now headed by Catholic monarchs, they set sail to the Americas, and over the period of about 300 years they gradually conquered and colonised large portions of North, Central and South America; killing or integrating the cultures of the native populations, and of course, amassing wealth in silver and gold and many other resources of these areas. They also managed to capture and subjugate cities in North Africa, and some smaller areas and islands in Asia and Oceania. The dominance of the Spanish Empire began to fall apart, as Spain suffered through its losses in the Napoleonic wars, and Spain's political structures and sovereignty wavered and came under scrutiny and pressure. Following on from these instabilities, Spain gradually lost all of its American territories through numerous wars of independence, and more final defeats of the Spanish by the United States.

Not long after the Spanish, then the French and British forces began their colonial expansions, often in direct competition with the Spanish and with each other. The French Empire expanded into large parts of North America and Canada and parts of the Caribbean, but they struggled to get a hold of South American territories, due to the Portuguese and Spanish already being established there. They also managed to establish some early holds in both India and Africa, and in Africa, they saw the great potential to secure the resources of certain foods and raw materials, and then to secure access to and control of the growing profitable slave trade.

Conflict with Britain severely damaged the initial French empire, and a second colonial push began after 1830, when France first invaded and conquered Algeria. They then moved in to establish holds on Morocco, invaded Tunisia, and built many colonies down through West and Equatorial Africa, and across to Madagascar. There were also ventures to expand into other areas within Asia, the Pacific islands, Cambodia and the Middle East. As political thinking changed, and later World Wars forced new alliances and treaties, so the calls for independence increased through the 20th century, eventually supporting decolonisation from France for the many nations and regions who voted to leave its colonial rule.

The British Empire began its first expansions late in the 16th century, with attempts to establish a colony in America; the first to become successfully established was called Jamestown (now part of Virginia in the USA). From these humble beginnings, and proposing that the natives of these other lands were uncivilised and needed British rule, language and religion, the British established about 13 colonies in North America for a time. However, these dominated colonies did not like the impositions of British rule, and gradually, through many battles of rebellion, and with support from the French and Spanish, they won their freedom and independence from the British.

This only spurred the British on to expand their Empire even further, to establish more of the wealth and power that would fuel further colonisations. They had established enforced control of most of India, and set up the East India company to exploit its workforces and generate wealth, spreading into other areas of Southeast Asia. Britain also made campaigns into Africa and enforced their rulership onto around thirty percent of the then African kingdoms and population, in various regions across the continent; again exploiting native labour and the natural resources of the lands, to build its imperial wealth and dominance. The British, along with other European colonisers around this time who had developed an inhumane philosophy of racial superiority, also had a large involvement in the transatlantic slave trade; forcibly migrating millions of Africans across Europe and the Americas, into impoverished slave labour.

At its height, the British Empire had control of areas across the entire globe: in North America and Canada, Central America and the Caribbean, parts of Africa, the Middle East, most of India and surrounding parts of Southeast Asia, some of Indonesia, Australia, New Zealand and the Pacific Islands. It is not until recently, after the Second World War, that the British empire and its controls started to decolonise and disband, due to changing political views of imperial control and domination, and the financial struggles that maintaining an empire could impose, especially after the losses incurred in such a major war. Gradually the colonies of the Empire established independence, or became part of an agreed commonwealth under new charters and agreements.

Around this period in history there were certainly many other imperial campaigns and numerous wars, transitions of power and changes in the controls of territories and resources; far too many to count and describe in a single chapter. There was a large Russian campaign, that came to dominate much of Asia and Eastern Europe for a time, later followed by the communist revolutions and establishment of the Soviet Union. There was a Japanese imperial campaign that reached its height in the early-mid 20th century, covering areas in China, Russia, Southeast Asia, Indonesia and the Pacific, before their historic surrender to the USA in 1945. There is also the American territorial expansion of what later became the USA, inflicting the conquering and enforced reservation restrictions upon the native Americans, and encouraging the settler colonisations of these previously free and indigenous lands. The USA forwarded a new sort of imperialism, or modern hegemony, where political and economic powers were grown with its nation's expansion, along with an extremely powerful and potentially dominant military force (to back it up), that could then put pressures and controls on other nations, to further its own economic interests and wealth.

So you've probably realised by now that I am no great scholar and protagonist of historic detail; I have really tried to avoid long lists of dates and specific battles here, in the truly extensive history of our warring human development. Yes, I will have barely scratched the surface of this history, and do genuinely appreciate that so much will have been omitted and missed out; my apologies if you have noticed the sometimes huge gaps, but there are already many encyclopaedias that document our history of wars, and you would perhaps need more than just one lifetime to study them all in any great detail. Hopefully, the little that I have linked together here, is enough to clarify the real point and focus of this chapter.

So what is it that I am actually trying to convey about this period of our continuing human history and development? What does this history show us, in its proliferation of wars and conflicts, its rise and fall of kingdoms and empires, its massacres of armies and peoples, and its establishments of rule, only to be followed by more wars and revolutions? What effect has all of this had on the formations of our cultures and the psychology of our thinking, regarding our social structures and their development and government, and also in respect of the imaginary national boundaries we have subsequently drawn up and sought to defend?

Humans have always instinctively sought to find places where food and shelter is readily available, and so had to compete to establish a hold in these provident territories. It may be easy just to glance over our history, even just to pick out the best bits and more positive progressions, and to say about the darker elements, 'well that's just the way it was back then'. But if we really look at it closely, and the immensity of all the violence, war and death, only then can we begin to get a realistic understanding of how it has affected the human psyche over the centuries, and the types of nations and societies we now live within. Nearly all of our modern day nations still fear war and domination to the extreme, that huge chunks of their national resources are poured into the developments of ever more destructive weapons, and into the building and maintenance of huge, battle ready armies and navies.

So what were the real instincts and instigations behind all of this historic violence? Where was the drive coming from, and what were its ultimate aims? To understand this we need only go back to our innate survival instincts to appreciate the source, and the often harsh violence of nature and of early human development. If we progress this and align this with the human desire to dominate and control more of the elements and resources that improve our survival, as repercussions of the fears of scarcity and suffering, then there are plenty of potential motivations for war as a means to gain power.

For collective groups, survival is generally the major incentive to stake their claim on lands and territories, and to follow the dictates of leaders, or to rebel. But for individuals, who may have won or fashioned positions of leadership and power, this can also drive an incentive to gain even more power and control, and to hoard resources and wealth; to become worshipped even, and live in positions of extreme luxury and privilege. Individuals who gained such positions of power, could then go on to convince themselves and their subjects, that this is righteous and justified, and that they are somehow more special and worthy of life and adoration.

Once greed had become established as a possible projection of the human mind and its psychology, two of the main elements that could enable its spread and development through human behaviours, were ruthless and ambitious leaders, and high numbers of supporting and subservient followers. As human populations rose and spread out over the last 4000 years of our history, so these two major elements were in abundance. Add these elements to the human desires to survive and become more prosperous, and you have the perfect breeding ground for greed within the populations of both of these elements: within the elite rich and leaders of our nations waging their war campaigns to gain more resources and living within privileged and lavish conditions, but also within the envy of the general populations, where individuals might see these privileges and start to want more for themselves.

These developing realities of class and division, that allowed greed to really take a hold of our human thinking and behaviours, and to spread through migrations of war to become set within the foundations of our societies, just needed the real power base of all human progress that is contained in the masses of the general populations, to continue to follow along and be subservient. So leadership controls and psychology continued to develop and adapt further as populations progressed, constantly looking at how best to continue to maintain this obedience.

Chapter 6: Social division, Indoctrination and Subjugation

For human societies to build up their strengths and numbers, and to be able to expand and make war with other groups to steal their territories and resources, then they need large, mostly willing populations: to work their large scale agriculture, to build and maintain their towns and cities, and, of course, to train in combat and become their armies, to the extremes that they would kill or die for their nation and its leaders. So how did humans create and maintain these social structures and beliefs, that could bring together, galvanise and maintain for the long term, such a workforce and large population of people, perhaps across many lands and territories? Especially when training as part of an army would raise the very real threat of a possibly violent and painful death in combat, which would definitely go against an individual's innate survival instincts.

If we go back to the first chapter of this book, and the core innate animal instincts in all humans, then one of these was described as 'self-survival'; so why use the prefix of 'self' here? Well I believe there is a subtle difference in the instincts of self-survival and more general species survival, which can become important as humans develop and evolve. As a primal animal instinct, then self, or selfish-survival, would put the individual's motivations to survive above everything else: if there is a threat, then the individual fights or runs (regardless of others in their group), if there is food, then the individual will eat all that it needs (regardless of whether others get to eat); self-survival, will act primarily in self interest. This behaviour can change though, within family and wider group living, especially when nurturing instincts come into play, or if the individual is convinced they have something more to fight for. If offspring or wider group members start to become viewed as extensions of our 'self', then we might act to fight and protect these as part of our survival instinct, perhaps even suffer or be killed in our attempts to defend them.

So while our original primal instincts may be self-survival, this survival instinct has the potential to expand and incorporate others. As humans have evolved psychologically, this survival instinct could potentially then be manipulated, trained to be overridden, and indoctrinated to incorporate ideologies even. This is extremely important in training and mobilising armies and their individual warriors or soldiers, and in motivating their premeditated marches to war and combat, where there is no initial direct and obvious threat to trigger the fight instincts of survival. The individuals have to be fully invested to put their lives on the line, they have to be convinced by what ever means ensures their subservience and loyalty, and there were many ways for those directing control to achieve such commitment and obedience.

The distinction of self-survival, over the instinct of a wider more general survival of a species as a whole, also becomes very important when considering the development of the imbalance of greed and its possible behaviours. It is only under a full commitment to survival of the individual 'self' alone, above all others within a social group, or indeed, above all other forms of life, that narcissistic and psychopathic psychologies then have the potential to develop and progress. This is at least one of the breeding grounds for the disease of greed to take a hold of thinking, and when there is no longer any care or thought for other life, but only for self gratifications, if such thinking is enabled power and control over others, then atrocities and environmental destruction can easily be actuated and progressed, without even a second thought or sign of conscience.

For this chapter though, we will primarily be looking at how ruling factions have developed and evolved techniques to secure their often selfish aims and positions of control, by convincing and controlling large populations of people to go to war for them and to accept their allotted roles within society, even if this means their suffering and acceptance of a lower class status. How do you override their survival instincts and convince the general populations to fight and possibly die inconsequentially, for a leader they may never even see, or to work and labour long hours, days, a lifetime, for some basic food and shelter, or to possibly suffer hardships and hunger when resources are scarce, while the elite ruling classes of your society live in extreme luxury; how could this be achieved and maintained for generation after generation over thousands of years ?

Well the truth is, such control wasn't always successful; the harsher the treatments and conditions of the general populations under their leaders, then the more likely there would be revolts and revolutions at some stage, and this has brought about the downfall of may nations and empires over the years. But for the most parts, although techniques and motivations have changed and evolved over the years, to adapt and stay on top of controlling large populations as they became more aware, then control and direction of the masses has succeeded to maintain the dictates of rulerships and their disparities over thousands of years of history, right up to our present day.

What follows are some of the most common techniques that have evolved and branched out over the centuries of human development, to be used by our leaders and ruling classes: social division between nations and peoples, to create the 'us versus them' scenarios; indoctrination, using various ideologies and religious manipulations; and subjugation, through repressed education and mental development, fear and threats of punishment, various forms of slavery, and the creation of dependencies by controlling essential resources. These were all given life through greedy and narcissistic minds and rulers, and so have come to infect, over time, the wider psychology of humanity.

Nearly all social groups throughout history: tribes, nations, empires, even republics (with 'elected' leaders), tended to have a sovereign leader or small set of ruling classes, usually followed by obedient lords and land owners and then generals and leaders of the armies (who all had to be kept close and loyal to the biddings of the rulers). There might also be religious leaders with influence, intermixed with these elite ruling classes, depending on the culture and the power that their religion had established over people. With the genus of a particular nation that is looking to be united and mobilised in its causes, then while social divisions will obviously exist between classes, often blatantly, it is better that these are subdued and kept distracted from focus to avoid discontent and dissent within the ranks, especially the higher populated, lower and military ranks. One way of doing this and of mobilising attacks on other societies and cultures, is to focus your nation's attentions upon and to escalate the social divisions and social differences with other tribes and nations; even to create the false notions of racial superiority.

So the first technique we are looking at in controlling populations' thinking and direction, and hopefully avoiding their deeper examination of any internal social inequalities, is to create and highlight more division between them and other neighbouring cultures and social groups (who may coincidentally have desirable lands and resources). This is about the social divisions between societies that will enable rulers to mobilise armies and the labour to maintain and feed them, and to motivate and justify their populations to go to war and fight and kill the peoples of other nations. It is about creating psychological divisions based on social differences between peoples and nations, both real and imagined, often concocted and exaggerated, to demonise the other side and dehumanise their image; to create the thinking that it is 'us versus them' for survival. And as a consequence, to create and encourage such thinking then perpetuates this type of thinking on both sides, that over prolonged periods of time and historical conflict, can lead to deep set enmities within rival populations.

    Establishing and building psychological divisions between societies usually relied upon highlighting and exaggerating the social differences between them: demonising their leaders, depicting their cultures and appearance as perhaps primitive and less worthy of rights, denouncing their gods as false and their religious practices as evil and against the true god /or gods of their own established religions and beliefs. Across the spectrum of comparison and judgement between cultures set to go to war, so these tactics would be used as justifications and motivations, on both sides, to rally the peoples and armies into killing each other and enforcing the other's surrender and subjugation. And if conflicts took place over many years and centuries between certain established cultures and opposing religious nations, then the judgements of rhetoric and rumour could become very deep seated in peoples psychology, causing long held racism and hatreds that would repeatedly trigger conflicts over and over again, throughout history and right up to the present day.

    While social divisions have often been blatant in their use to condemn and attack other cultures, all of these tactics of control have also evolved and developed over the centuries to branch out and achieve their aims in more subtle ways. Some tactics of social division within a society have been used by the ruling classes to identify and quell threats to their power and control from within, especially against minority groups who might start to speak out against their leaders and to raise the interest of the general populations. Creating negative disinformation and judgements about such minorities, or finding ways to condemn them as political or religious law breakers (and so to imprison or destroy them), were powerful tactics that could be used by leaders and their advisors. As they held the powers to be able to set laws and to speak out to the masses, and later to control most educational frameworks and forms of general media within their societies, then such tactics were often easy to implement.

There are a whole host of social divisions that were set within our cultures through history, mostly to manipulate and control the thinking and direction of populations, and many of these are still in play today. Divisions based on wealth and privilege, class, intellect, race, creed and colour, ideology, lifestyles, sexuality, gender; the list goes on and on, especially as we have become more socially diverse as a race. Even now, with the immense potentials of what we could achieve as one common and unified human race working together, we have not come remotely close to resolving our numerous differences that cause ongoing conflict. Partly because they have become so well established over the centuries, but mainly because we are still being dominated by our primitive animal instincts of fear. This has lead to the control of greed growing and becoming more established in so many of our governmental structures, to continue to be kept alive and championed in its modern forms by so many of our leaders and corporations.

Although social divisions and dictated judgements between nations are a useful tactical way to controlling people's thinking, a big element to these becoming set within mass populations, to further control their actions and reactions, is the use of the tactic of indoctrination. Once you have set the tone of your societies more righteous political and religious beliefs, and declared the wrongful differences that other nations support and uphold; the next thing you need to be able to do is to strongly implement these thoughts within your peoples minds: to indoctrinate them and get them to believe that these are actually their fundamental beliefs, so that they will judge and act almost instinctively upon them. So this is the next stage of maintaining divisions for conflict and empire building: to successfully develop mass forms of indoctrination within your social structures.

Indoctrination, the process of teaching or enforcing others to accept a set of beliefs uncritically, also has an extremely long period of development within our human history, and many, both blatant and more subtle ways, of being implemented and imposed. It may be that it began more as cultural identification, with ancestral remembrances around the camp fires and stories of hunting and rival conflicts of the past, where the ways and aggressions of other tribes might be highlighted if they were a continued threat. But as societies expanded and became more settled, and leaders became more premeditated in how they could control and direct their subjects, then stories and rumours could be manipulated and spread to support their leaders' agendas.

Indoctrination has grown through many forms and guises within our social leadership practices. There has been historical indoctrination - teaching one sided history according to supporting your own nation's righteousness in the past, and the lack of integrity and evil nature of its enemies. Political indoctrination - through social structures that instilled that labour and tribute (taxes) for the monarch and the realm was just and honourable (and punishable if refused), and through general glorification of leaders and their empire and its campaigns to expand, but also with the promises that life under such powerful leaders and empires would provide privilege and protection. Military indoctrination - through repetitive training from a young age, to instil obedience and loyalty to an infallible ruler, and to encourage you to fight unquestionably for your monarch, nation and fellow citizens. Religious indoctrination - depending on the religion and number or type of gods, people might be lead to believe their fates lay in the hands of their religion and its god / gods, and that their leaders may be chosen by their gods, or even that their leaders may be gods themselves to be worshipped and followed. And, finally, ideological / peer indoctrination - where certain sets of beliefs are passed on from generation to generation, family to family, peer to peer, and where common beliefs are held within a culture, like the glory of dying in battle for example, that were an individual to question or oppose, they might become ostracised.

Indoctrination on a mass scale is never really an easy process, as it requires the populations involved to be convinced, to possibly suffer hardships, and to act, even die for, sometimes cruel and despotic omnipotent leaders. There are, however, many tactics that can be used to help the implanting of indoctrinations and its continued maintenance and growth, once established in the collective mind. The first tool that is often used is fear, as this is a common instinct to all humans and so should affect the widest range of people. Fear can be used in many ways to keep populations inline and to go along with the directed agendas of rule. Threats that you might lose your land and resources if you do not get behind your leader and help to destroy its enemies; threats that you might be imprisoned, tortured or killed if you stand out and disagree with the general consensus being proposed; threats of starvation, threats to your family's wellbeing and threats to your future bloodline. These are some of the basic threats of fear that can be used to stop people questioning, and to ensure they accept what they are told.

The indoctrination of religion over recent millennia, and the use of religious induced fear or indignation, has been a widely used tool for dominating and controlling the behaviours of populations. Firstly, the religion, of cultural origins or perhaps newly adopted, had to become set within the thinking and acceptance of the general population, often with repetitive indoctrination and possible threats to those who resisted. If the general population of the culture became fully accepting of its religion, and could be convinced that their God was the most righteous, and perhaps, that the religious leaders in power were the mouth pieces for their God, then religious dictates and commands might become followed without question. This could be further instilled and enforced, if it was taught that refusing the religious instruction and commands of leaders would be going against their God, which could incur misfortune, wrath or eternal damnation.

If their God was depicted as all seeing and omnipotent, then nothing might escape its knowing, and people could be kept in fear of unrighteous actions or challenges to authority. Also, if other cultures and their religions could be painted as worshipping false idols and following wicked practices that were offensive to their culture's God, then populations could be incited into indignation and more easily directed into wars and campaigns of colonisations, under the pretext of religious offence. Some of these religious judgements and conflicts have become so deep set in certain culture's psychology over hundreds or thousands of years, that they still incite indignation and conflict to this day. Of course, once religion is set as a base control for the psychology of large populations, then there is great scope for many ideals, judgements and social expectations to be introduced, to control peoples actions and behaviours, which is why it has been so widely adopted and used by ruling classes and leaders.

The tactic of 'problem and solution' is another tool that is popular to unite thinking and encourage the acceptance of direction, as it can help to build trust between the ruling government and its populations. It works by first highlighting 'problems', real or fabricated, to the general populations: marauders may be coming from the east, certain crops may become scarce if the rainfall is low, we need to build the fortifications and size of our city's palace for better protection. Once the problem is made known and the fear is circulated, then the direction of state leadership presents itself as offering the strong and viable solution: we must unite more and build our trained, obedient armies up, to defend against these marauders if they come (or perhaps to go and attack them first); we must have more labourers working the land for crops and to build more irrigation to increase food production; we must have more labour and work more hours in hard conditions, to ensure the city's protection.

Each time the problem is presented to raise fear and worry in the population, so the solution can be galvanising and motivating, even if the aims of rulers or government may have had different agendas sometimes: they wanted to attack certain lands to the east for their resources; they wanted to increase food stocks to feed a bigger army; the emperor wanted a bigger palace built in his honour. These are very simple examples to illustrate the point, and while not all the problems will be manipulative, the 'problem / solution' tactics are widely used to direct the public's thinking and actions in ways that best suits the aims of the ruling classes, but keeps the public invested and on side. This is still very commonly used to this day: raise problems and distribute media that induce fear, then offer your government solutions, or commercial solutions, that might appease and resolve that fear.

Probably one of the most premeditated and powerful tactics for indoctrination that has grown and evolved through our societies, is the control of the agendas of education and media output. While education across the wider populations may not have been extensive and widespread in our earlier societies, there would have been teaching passed down through generations, and public announcements and information passed on to the wider populations. The more the ruling classes could dictate and control these narratives, then the more they could direct thinking and behaviours and to set these within the foundations of their social orders, and the less likely there would be dissent or revolt. As time progressed and social functions became more advanced and widespread, then controlling the education of generations from the earliest of ages upwards, would be a potent way of setting your agendas within their minds and controlling the development of their thinking for long term obedience and unity.

Controlling the contents of the different forms of media would be vitally important to direct or sway the publics thoughts, attentions and actions, or to quell any discontent before it grew and spread. Controlling media output has been a strong focus of particularly dictatorial regimes, to tightly restrict people's free thinking and implant the agendas of their leaders. Depending on the intensity and frequency with which such manifestos and propaganda are delivered to the public, then media control has always walked a close line alongside brain washing, from the obviously and oppressively blatant, right down to the subtle more hidden and manipulative tactics. Religion, when working in agreements with the ruling classes, would also often be tied into these aims, using inquisitions to try to wipe out contentious beliefs and practices, banning certain behaviours, or condemning and destroying certain types of literature. It would also advocate the principle of divine rule; teaching that their literature and commands were the truly righteous direction and must always be studied and followed above all others.

As types of media and communication have grown and expanded into our modern age, then new tactics have had to evolve, as it proved more and more difficult to control the agendas of the many expanding channels of the media, and of the numerous different ideals and belief systems evolving and spreading. One way has been to try to assert more control, as exposed through more recent forms of dictatorial communism, where agendas are strict, other ideals are demonised, and populations are cut off more from the influences of the rest of the world.

This has proved more challenging though as time progressed and communication systems quickly became more easily accessible and harder to police, and people became more questioning and enquiring. So another modern tactic that has developed is the 'flooding' of media with masses of information and disinformation from all sorts of sources, beliefs and extremes. This then creates conflicting information and potential confusion, where it becomes increasingly more difficult to know what the truth is and which source to trust, or where government advocates can play off the different types of disinformation to profess that only they offer the 'true' information and solutions.

Confusion through the mass flooding of the media also presents another widely used tactic, to enable already established indoctrination to continue to go unnoticed and unquestioned, and perhaps, for hidden agendas to pass through the system, disguised as false information in the mass sea of disinformations. You can start to see just from the last sentence how easily things can begin to seem confusing; what's real and what is disinformation can quickly become entangled and confused. This can only add to the tactics of distraction as a whole: keeping peoples' minds and time always occupied with theory and counter theory, humour and trivia, hopes and imaginations. Distraction of the general populations has gradually evolved over the centuries into huge modern day forms of media and entertainment. In early societies it might be used to distract from rising discontent and to raise public moral, through large public holidays and competitive tournaments, or plays depicting previous leaders glorious lives and victories, or religious ceremonies and agendas. All of these could also help to reinforce the controlled agendas of education and propaganda.

In our more modern societies, then distraction and occupation of the mind can be found everywhere: in drugs and alcohol, mass competitive sports and entertainments media, endless social media and wealth and celebrity indoctrinated worship, the daily occupation of work and careers, and in the ever increasing array of financial commitments and responsibilities. An occupied and distracted mind is usually a less enquiring and questioning mind, as it has less time for research and contemplation. This we will expand upon and look at more in later chapters, as it all ties in with the modern controls and channels of greed.

Another basic psychological tactic of indoctrination, used from early childhood and through all ages, is that of 'praise and reward' or just 'promise' of reward. Promise of reward is quite simple and is used everywhere in societies, right up to our modern day political canvassing and campaigning: 'if you accept my rule and dictates' or 'if you vote in my party and its agendas', then I will offer you these rewards and privileges, or you will benefit in these ways by the things that I do and achieve as your leader. All very simple psychological techniques, but they work effectively again and again, especially if you deliver at least some of what you promise as a leader.

Praise and reward can be a bit more of a long term and manipulative tactic, often used in childhood to control and direct behaviours, but once established, its behaviours can become very deep set and hard to identify and change. It works best by repeated consistency: 'if you act in this desired way', or 'if you do what I ask and want', then I will be happy and grateful, and I will praise you and give you these treats or privileges. Whereas 'if you do not do what I ask and want', then you will not have these privileges and may be chastised and punished. Again, initially very simple, but very effective psychological programming, especially if done constantly over a period of time. It is a technique that can adapt and tailor its methods for individuals and groups, according to their needs and desires and the subsequent rewards that are offered.

One last major tactic that was progressively used throughout our history in supporting elements of indoctrination, was the creation and development of iconography. In our earlier cultures, stories of human icons, usually heroic warriors, explorers or leaders, were told alongside the stories of the gods, detailing their super human like exploits, victories and achievements, and sometimes to even elevate humans to god like figures. Such stories, passed on through generations, progressed and expanded into images and sculptures in some cultures, and as these icons become more ingrained in a cultural psyche, so they would dictate to a degree, the type of cultural qualities for general populations to look up to and admire and emulate.

    This indoctrination has taken place right up to our present day modern societies, where we have a whole host of iconic figures, painted and presented to us as desirable to emulate (even to worship in our behaviours). These can be very revealing as to what our societies may be presenting and encouraging, to greater or lesser degrees, as images and behaviours to admire; modern social medias are now full of information, articles and news coverage, on the excessively rich and famous, the self-made multi-millionaire or billionaire, as these things attempt to hold aloft the excesses of greed and inequality, as desirable aspects of success in our societies. This might then encourage us to accept such extreme disparities, and perhaps to even seek and believe we have the right to gain more for ourselves, regardless of the possible slave labour and pollution that might be enabled in creating such extreme wealth, or in funding such elite lifestyles.

    With the current mass of diversities across the many cultures of our world, there are now many types of icons that we have created and look up to, both positive and negative, humanitarian and destructive, loving and greedy. This particular brief example is just to illustrate how certain iconic figures can actually be pushed more through media control, to help indoctrinate acceptance, even admiration, of certain lifestyles and beliefs, even if they may be detrimental to wider humanity. All mass media is performing some form of advertising to the general public; whether it's in the tone and balance of their news stories, the contents of their informations and disinformations, or in the blatant marketing of mass produced goods for consumerism; all media has something to say and to sell.

Working alongside forms of indoctrination, and often intermixed, there are also many varying methods of subjugation being used to better enable the control and direction of mass populations and their cultures. Subjugation would need to be employed over two main types of population: those already within the society who need to be maintained control of and to restrict any possible rebellions, and those recently conquered or colonised, to find ways to integrate them into the now victorious culture, and to become subservient and productive if possible. So again, different tactics of subjugation would need to be used, according to where the people were at in their social compliances: from the blatant threat of torture and death, to the subtle hidden repressions of education and free, unbiased information.

Subjugation within organised societies usually takes on more subtle forms, for if the laws and regimes become too obviously oppressive, or create too much widespread hardship and suffering, this can often lead to uprisings and rebellions. Internal disputes and civil wars are never good outcomes when trying to build strong unity or expanding empires. One of the main ways to subjugate the peoples of your own society is to ensure that they are dependants: as a leader with large obedient armies at your disposal, if you and your chosen lords officially own the lands and control the resources essential for life - food stocks, water and the right to build shelters and homes, then the threat of losing these things is perhaps the strongest incentive to people staying in line and accepting the rule of authority with little or no question. If you also control the political systems, and the general populations have no say, then your power cannot be challenged or taken away, and rulerships can be continued on through bloodlines, where the same rules and agendas are passed on through families and aristocracies, as well as lands, titles and deeds.

Internal societal subjugation needs to avoid dissent and revolution, so it can often develop to restrict the opportunities of its peoples to progress and possibly become more independent. Controlling and restricting education has been used to stop people becoming more literate and aware, and so communicating ideas to challenge conditions. Keeping them relatively poor is also another financial subjugation, as they are forced to spend most of their time and energies working, to feed and house themselves and their families, leaving little time for political contemplations or for organising realistic mass revolutions, if they feel heavily repressed.

Religion, as mentioned earlier, has offered a whole other, long term dimension to on-going subjugation, for if you can instil and control religious belief and fear across a whole society, and convince them that going against their leaders dictates is going against their god/gods, then you can get people to do almost anything. Throughout our more recent human history there have been religions purporting to be about love, forgiveness and human fellowship, but, when directed by religious leaders more focused on power and empire building, in the name of these religions based on love, they have actually been able to convince their followers to go out and kill other people on a grand scale. There really is no greater contradiction and extreme of subservience, than a religion based on love, directing its followers to actively go out and kill other people. This just shows you what the psychological control of indoctrination, subjugation and subservience can enable.

When it comes to the subjugation of conquered peoples and nations, then the challenges become even more difficult: these people may have long held enmities with their new leaders and dominant culture, they may have been at war for some time, and they may have strong wills and never wish to capitulate or be subservient. These elements will usually decide what approach is then taken: if they are truly stubborn and steadfast to their own cultures, then military force may be the only repression that works and the threat of slaughter or execution if they are captured. Slavery was another popular option for some conquering societies, but this could be costly and potentially dangerous, for the prisoners would have to be fed and accommodated, and, if they were to escape, they might turn on you and kill you at the first opportunity. Trying to 'break' captives was also a tactic used, with torture, hardships and starvation, but this again could be time consuming and dangerous, and when the will is broken, there might not be much left that is human and able to be productive.

However, if the conquered culture had genuinely surrendered under negotiations or military threats, or become tired and depleted by war, then they could possibly become more compliant to cultural integration and subservience. They might have to accept the removal of their old religious practices and beliefs for those of their new culture, and they may be forced to swear loyalty, give up lands and resources and become dependants or tax payers to their new leaders. If the alternative is death however, then subservience would always be a preferred option for many, at least until they could possibly come up with a better plan, and raise new armies and allegiances.

The Romans were one imperial conquering culture renowned for adapting their methods of subjugation and the integration of other cultures. While they had strong powerful armies and military might and experience, they developed the skills of political debate and negotiations, realising that this could be a much less destructive and costly way of subjugating and integrating cultures and of maintaining their allegiance. They would establish treaties and agreements, allowing cultures to keep many of their beliefs and practices, perhaps taking and using some of these cultures best inventions, but also introducing some of their own societal organisation and skills. While the integrated culture may now have Roman rule and outposts established, and have to swear allegiance to Rome and pay tributes, they could continue to live on and work their lands in perhaps milder, less oppressive subservience, compared to complete domination and cultural displacement.

      To sum up the elements of this chapter a little, in relation to how thoughts and actions of greed were enabled to expand through human behaviours and controls of society; what was clearly present and dominant throughout all developing societies and cultures throughout our history, was large divides between the wealthy ruling classes controlling resources and armies, and the poorer masses of the general populations doing their biddings, and agreeing or being forced to be subservient. These smaller elite groups of ruling classes, lords and aristocracy, under the extreme psychologies of power, dominance and control, often became 'infected' with the psychological imbalances of greed that extreme power and dominance can encourage: inflated visions of their importance and greatness (desiring reverence and worship), desires to ever expand their control, dominance and empires, desires to build up and hoard more and more wealth, riches and resources, desires to live in extreme luxury, palatial splendour and to build monuments of their greatness, and the desires to continue their bloodlines of control, by maintaining their sovereign positions of power.

      Such extreme and unbalanced human desires, becoming dominant in the minds of many of those in power who ultimately were directing whole societies, could often mean, in the single minded commitment to achieving and maintaining their desires, a loss of care or respect for other life on a grand scale. This is repeatedly exposed throughout our history of violent wars, imperial campaigns and colonisations, all accounting for incredible numbers of human slaughters and deaths over the centuries. It is also exposed in how general populations have been viewed and manipulated over the centuries by their leaders: controlled by premeditated tactics of division, indoctrination and subjugation, to keep peoples repressed, subservient and compliant.

With greed's expanding disregard for other human life and their rights to live freely, then this disregard for life continued to progress further as we moved into times of industrial revolution and modern capitalism. Now the life of nature, its environments and eco-systems, would become increasingly disregarded and under attack, all for the insatiable desires of the fuels and raw materials of production, that would enable greed its ultimate aims, of unlimited personal profiteering and controls in every aspect of society.

Chapter 7: The Industrial Revolutions and Modern Imperialism

While wars and conflicts still continue to this day between some cultures and nations, as the imperial conquests and colonisations had spread out over the entire globe, and regions and nations began to establish more permanent boundaries and treaties, then attentions gradually turned more to commerce, human invention and systems of government and finance. War has certainly never moved far from human threats of force and dominance between nations, and some of the biggest world wars have been fought between groups of nations over just the last few centuries, but our more established nations, along with their vast military forces, all gradually started to invest more time and energy into industry.

Military power and the building and maintenance of large armed forces, is still a huge part of most modern day nations' planning and spending, and the continued progression of the 'arms race', aiming to build ever more powerful and destructive weapons, has always developed alongside the more domestic aspects of the industrial revolutions. Just how destructive our invented weapons could become was devastatingly realised in the use of the first atomic bombs upon Japan in 1945; a warning to the entire human race of the dark directions we were investing in. In general though, the establishment and greater stability of our national boundaries, to form more defined countries, states and republics, has afforded much more time, money and energy to progress other aspects of human creativity and endeavour.

Following on from the many positive progressions of the Renaissance period in Europe, between the 14th and 17th centuries, where there were many developments in art, architecture and literature, and in philosophy and medicine; it was the development of scientific knowledge in particular, through trial and observation, conclusions and documentation, that began to offer the inventive and commercial worlds of human endeavour ever more practical and adaptable raw materials, elements and fuels, and ever more ingeniously created machineries and types of transport and communication. Although this was happening in smaller pockets around the world, with the discovery of new scientific knowledge and the developments of new and ingenious inventions, the real push, on a larger industrial scale, began with Britain's expanding economy in around 1760 and gradually spread across Europe and later on to the United States and parts of Asia.

The main elements of the initial Industrial Revolution, centred around a combination of new resources and ingenuity: new types of fuels and their engines, new stronger metallic raw materials for building, new machineries (first for textiles production primarily, but progressively for almost every kind of production), new large scale organisation of labour and factory environments, and new and improving types of transportation and communication systems. All of these elements developing together, with society now more stable and focused on its social improvements and trade, gave rise to a rapid explosion of industrial development that has never really stopped growing ever since.

With the gradual depletion of wood for fuel in Great Britain, so the mining of coal as a major fuel source began to increase. As these early coalfields were developed near waterways, then the coal could be more easily transported around the country, and as mining techniques were improved, it become clear that resources of coal were abundant in areas of Britain. Sources of lighting that had been developed around this time, were run on coal gas, and coke (developed while refining coal through high temperatures) was needed in the new developing productions of iron and then steel, the two major materials that began to be in demand on a grand scale for construction and the building of machinery. As the mining of coal was already well established within Britain, along with a good distribution network, then this put them significantly ahead of the rest of Europe regarding industrial development, as the use of iron and steel and of various engines and mechanical inventions all began to expand rapidly.

Higher demand for coal, iron and steel, forced extraction and production methods to expand and become industrialised, and for a whole host of chain reactions in development to progress: the progression of the steam engine, in running machinery and new forms of transportation; the expansion of canal systems, to transport coal and other goods for industry; the expansion of rail networks, for transporting goods and then people; coal gas burnt for lighting and then cooking; expanded production and use of machinery for increased agricultural production; the rise of large organised factory production methods, fuelled by coal and driven by demand, and then there also came the development of the use of electricity and petroleum, and the invention of the internal combustion engine. It truly was a perfect storm of new available fuels and materials, inventive thinking and increasing human demand for expansion and progress.

Everything in our human societies was moving away from the intensive labour time of working the land by hand and crafting individual items by hand, and gradually being transitioned to industrial, mechanical and manufactured production methods. This, of course, needed ever increasing amounts of fuel, and demanded larger and larger factories and production lines. More agricultural production and more transportation networks, lead to more food availability and more variety of foods, some of which were now beginning to be processed and more preservable. With more food available, so populations began to rise, and industrialisation as a whole supported a more rapid population growth across the entire human world.

In respect of this almost exponential population growth, we went from reaching the population of our first billion, in around 1800, to doubling this to our second billion by the late 1920s. We had then doubled up again to four billion by the mid 1970s, and have doubled this again to eight billion by the year 2022. With a slightly slower but continuing population rise, and increasing environmental abuse and climate instabilities, then providing sustainably for our ever growing populations is becoming increasingly more difficult; something we will look into more later, as we assess the challenges that extreme capitalism and greed have come to present to our current societies.

Another human institution that developed and grew power and influence over our industrialised nations and their economies, was the expansion of the concept of banking into dedicated banking systems and companies. Banking organisations were split into two main categories: the central banks, responsible for regulating the finances and stabilities of a government or group of countries (safeguarding gold reserves, setting interest rates, issuing bank notes and coins, and keeping an eye on and reacting to all sorts of financial risks and possible instabilities), and the independent or commercial banks, run solely for making profit, who, using the monies deposited by the general public and companies, then utilised this money, to invest and make loans with added interest charges, and by buying and selling resources at a profit.

Strangely, not all central banks were owned and controlled by their governments, which might have ensured better reinvestment of all monies and profits back into government and public improvements. For the first 250 years of its existence, for example, the Bank of England was a private bank owned by shareholders, so personal profits and monies could be taken out by the shareholders. This has become the common practice throughout all banking systems and most established businesses over the years: to prioritise profit, and through investors, board members and share holders, to enable personal profiteering that is disproportionate to need, often restricting the wider advantages of better reinvestment for the general public. Of course, those involved in developing and controlling our banking and monitory systems were enabled to develop the economics that worked in their favour, and you will probably never have heard of any stories of a bank owner who is not extremely wealthy.

Throughout many of our societies around the world, social systems have developed to make us more dependant on banking services: how we are paid, how we buy and sell goods, how businesses must manage their money, the costs of living that dictate we may need mortgages and loans for homes and vehicles etc. And all the while, the more of other peoples' money that banks have and can use, then the more profit they can make for themselves, and the more disproportionate their earnings and bonuses can become. If none of this profiteering is technically illegal, then there's no way of stopping it, as desire for profit so often has superseded morality in an extreme capitalist psychological environment. Wherever large amounts of monies or resources are in play or being moved around, then you will find the financial vultures, looking for ways to siphon off a percentage for themselves, hoping this won't be noticed as they live off the labour of others.

Alongside and intertwined with all of these industrial expansions and developments, a new entrepreneurial thinking and focus on consumerism began to grow, and this thinking gradually rose to spearhead the industrial revolutions now spreading across the world, in what was called the second Industrial Revolution, beginning around 1870 onwards. Economies were changing worldwide, and although it was often slow, general wealth and living standards were improving for most western populations. Changing politics and manifestos adapted to accommodate the expansions of industrialisation; workers were trained and became more skilled in large scale materials extractions, factory operations and mass production techniques, and they progressively fought to create more union rights for their pay, working hours and conditions. Gradually, all our economies and resource controls were becoming dominated by industrialisation and commercialism.

So what are some of the common repercussions that can be highlighted from this brief overview of the huge expansions taking place through the industrial revolutions, and where did greed fit in to all of this? On the one side, standards of living were gradually improving for most populations, at least in the western world; while populations were increasing, so was food productions and diversity, standards of housing and sanitation, and the rights to vote and influence your choice of government. While to begin with industrialisation often meant long and hard hours of work for labour forces, in mines and potentially dangerous factory environments, under the strict control of wealthy owners who might even abuse the labour of women and children for very little reward…, gradually, through progressively built democratic unions, these conditions were challenged and legally improved. So, on the surface, there was much that was noticeably changing for the better for general populations.

As commercial enterprises increased everywhere, and banks grew in their wealth and social involvements, it was identified that the idea of more income for general populations, which might include some 'disposable' income, would boost both commercial spending and demand, as well as increase the monies that the banks would have to utilise for their profits. And if people did not immediately have the money to spend and consume, the banks would increasingly offer loans and monies borrowed against agreed assets. So loans would either be repaid with significant added interest, or, if payments were defaulted, then assets could be seized and sold; either way, the Banks would nearly always come out on top. These modern elements of increased income and the issuing of loans and credit, whilst causing a boom in consumerism and the materialism of general populations, has been the main fuel to allowing the extreme over-developments of industry and production, and all of the damages this has then done to our environments.

And now we come to the real downsides to industrialisation, mass production and consumerism; the things that are never well advertised, and often kept hidden from the general populations, or, at least, played down and distorted. The first and most obvious byproducts of large scale industrial production are waste and pollution; elements that societies have struggled with throughout this whole period of history and right up to the present day, and ones that have only gotten worse, as industrialisation has continually expanded and spread. So let us look at some of the worst elements of waste and pollution that are direct results of industrialisation, and also at the environmental damage caused by increased materials extractions, irresponsible waste disposal methods and mass pollution.

There are environmental damages done with almost every type of mining and materials harvesting: fossil fuels, wood, precious metals, gemstones, base elements and minerals for example, and with the expansions of industrialisation, the lists of individual raw materials that were being traced, cut down or dug out of the Earth are truly extensive. Large scale mining for industrial uses is a big operation, as lands have to be tested and drilled for adequate amounts of the desired materials, or dug out on a trial basis to see if they are present. Once found, then large scale labour forces are required for working the mines, machinery and tools and various transportation networks. Mining techniques can vary depending on the ease of access and the material required; from huge open mines, that may use explosives to open up the land and reveal materials, to extremely deep and long mining shafts, buried deep underground.

If we look at coal as an initial example of the scope of damages that can be done, then there are lots of wastes in the separation of coal and other substances: waste coal and mine waste (mixtures of soil and rock with coal), and liquid coal waste (acidic mine run off and toxic waste water from washing coal in preparation for burning). Then there is waste and pollution produced when burning coal for all its different uses: coal ash or coal combustion waste (containing large quantities of toxic materials that are often put into landfill or impoundments - now sometimes polluting ground water sources), large carbon dioxide omissions (affecting the chemical balance of our air quality and atmosphere, and subsequently our climate), and 'scrubber sludge' (produced in trying to absorb and control air pollution when burning coal, especially sulphur dioxide, which leaves a wet solid 'sludge' that needs to be safely stored or disposed of).

I have used the extraction and production of coal here, as just one brief example, as there have been constant air quality issues due to its industrialised use, especially around built up areas when atmospheric conditions reduce air movement. But with every fossil fuel use (coal, crude oil and natural gas) and all raw material extraction processes for industrial production, of which there are now far too many to list in one small chapter, then there are significant waste products and byproducts of pollution, all going into the land and atmosphere, or having to be disposed off or stored somewhere. Combine these altogether over several hundred years of constant expansion in industrial production, for massively increasing populations, and you have a worldwide waste and pollution problem, now affecting eco-systems and climates in a manner that is almost too big to comprehend and face up to. So it just continues to go on, and we will examine this more later when looking at the current realities of our human world.

Another of the real downsides to the ever increasing use of natural resources to fuel continual expansions of mass production, is that finite resources will all eventually dwindle and run out (most fossil fuels are predicted to be running low by the year 2050), and replenishable resources may simply not be able to keep up with growing production demands. If you then combine this increasing expansion of demand with the already existing elitist controls of lands, resources and financial systems, and with the enabled opportunity for the generation of ever increasing profits in mass production, for the few in control…, then the psychology of greed was given a huge field of potential to expand its reign and dominate economic thinking in modern human societies.

The new economic powers of the biggest and fastest developing countries, and their growing corporate controls of labour forces and resources, then initiated and accelerated the movements of modern economic imperialism: the race to find, exploit and take control of all the new resources and fuels needed for mass production and for expanding transport networks; the race to set up more factories and production lines, with the cheapest mass labour that could be found; and the race to generate and expand the demand and markets for every product imaginable, by capturing and directing the attentions of the mass populations of potential consumers. When profit becomes the priority focus above everything else, then greed can completely take over the thinking of its champions..., and so, worldwide capitalism, in all of its many guises and disguises, has been given full reign for a time.

Chapter 8: Capitalism - The Disguise and 'Normalisation' of Greed

Where do we begin with the definition and understanding of capitalism? While we may briefly look at the theoretical pros and cons of capitalism, and I am not an advocate for what it has been doing to our societies and planet, this chapter is certainly not a personal campaign against capitalist politics. This chapter will endeavour to look at the two main aspects of capitalism: the political theory and rhetoric of capitalism in how it has affected our thinking and behaviours, and the actual realities of the extremes of capitalism, in how it has affected our communities and societies, and the natural world that we depend upon for our survival.

Capitalism is defined as: an economic and political system in which property, business and industry are controlled by private owners rather than by the state, with the purpose of making profit. This definition actually says quite a lot already, and you can immediately see a potential breeding ground for the disease and imbalanced thinking of greed: individuals, or small groups of organised individuals, owning large proportions of property, land, business and industry, with growing controls over economic and political systems. But capitalism, in theory, does not necessarily have to equate to the imbalances of greed, which is why it has been able to sell itself to mass populations. If it is managed and controlled fairly, and profit and wealth is shared out equally and reinvested in improving societies and communities, then on paper at least, it can seem quite a beneficial proposition. This is one of the balances that those upholding the controls of capitalism have always tried to create the illusion of.

It is only when the thinking and desire for profit becomes the primary focus and ultimate aim of success, to facilitate the amassing of personal wealth and the elite privileges this can then enable, that thinking can become distorted into imbalances of greed and the extremely disproportionate sharing and use of wealth and resources. Profit is defined as: money that is earned in trade or business after the costs of producing and selling goods and services are taken into account. So if all the costs of producing and selling are covered in trade, extraction, transportation, manufacture, running costs and fair living wages for all involved, then why is there actually a need for profit? Well maybe some reasonable increase in the final price set for items could be good, if it can all be reinvested into better, cleaner, more efficient and technologically improved production. But where did this need and justification for personal profiteering come from? Why did it become common behaviour and privilege, for those controlling resources, production and prices, to just add more profit into the equation for the sole purpose of boosting their own personal wealth, beyond a fair living wage? Well the simple answer is, there was nothing to stop those in control, so they simply helped themselves, again and again and again.

The basic ideals of capitalism had been there throughout the ages, as we have explored, it is there in our primitive animal genetics and fears: to compete for resources, to dominate and control, to improve our own selfish chances of survival. And so it went on through elite ruling classes and aristocracies, who would build up, live with and control hoards of wealth and resources, and try to maintain control of compliant and willing armies and populations. But now, through establishing capitalism within the political foundations of society's thinking and economic systems, advocates could create and protect their own legal controls and justifications for personal profiteering; often disguised as profit for the greater good, but the realities tell a different story over time. Capitalism is primitive competition, taken into modern economics: it pits person against person, business against business and nation against nation, and, as with nearly all competition, there is usually one, or a small minority of winners, along with a much larger majority of losers. Your only friends in the capitalist mind set of business are the ones that can support you making profits; everyone and everything else is of little or no consequence.

So those in control at the heads of our industries, banks and corporate businesses, galvanised and championed capitalism as the best basis for economic growth and success, and as the basis for strong governments and finance. They rubbed shoulders with, influenced, donated to, or actually became, the ministers of such capitalist governments, for this is where the long term control would come from to protect their interests. Even if the labour forces and establishing unions could see and challenge the disparities of what was really happening with profits and control; lengthy political debates, bribery, small gestures and influences would persist to placate or distract them while business continued.

In reality, the entire world and most of our general populations' livelihoods were becoming so tied into and dependant upon the controls of industry and capitalist economies, that almost every political party of influence, that could afford to present themselves to be voted in, could not be separated from capitalism; it was just about the differences in how they would distribute wealth and what they promised to deliver to the people. Most democratic political parties that developed through this time, as voting rights became more widespread, were aligned with industrialisation simply because it had become so dominant and central to our existence and living economies, which, by their inseparable association, meant that capitalism was pulling all of the strings.

This is how capitalist ideals became firmly rooted in our modern society's psychology; the pretty pictures were presented and sold to us all, and even if we thought our political views were against it, we would nearly all be working for it and supporting it in some way, as it was running nearly all our commerce, business and essential living provisions. Capitalism promised much to the peoples of the world: free markets where the individual could decide their own fate; competition, encouraging innovation and cheaper, better services; more equal opportunity and freedom to produce and sell; buyers now deciding by demand the type of goods produced; more products, more services and more choice; and, of course, more profit, money and wealth for all…, all leading to a healthy, wealthy, more equal, educated, civilised society.

It all sounds wonderful, who wouldn't want a slice of that, and for some, in small groups or for short periods, some of these promises have been realised. However, to get a truly honest view and perspective of capitalism, and to how it has affected our world, then it has to be viewed fully in context in relation to its direct and indirect repercussions, and to how it has affected thinking and behaviours in humans. We live in a finite world, with finite amounts of resources, so there is only so much pie to go around; even if we keep making more and bigger pies, there is a limit to how much there is to share. So if people are encouraged and told it is their free right to keep seeking a bigger slice for themselves, then somewhere along the line, others are going to lose a share or miss out completely. To be able to keep building upon your share, you need to be kept ignorant of the damaging repercussions, or to become devoid of feeling and compassion, so as to hide from or ignore them. These are two of the actions that extreme capitalist thinking has encouraged over the years, and which have also allowed it to continue to go on for so long, unchallenged by a greater majority.

Another thing that capitalism set out to achieve through its advocates, at least in some more economically powerful western societies, was to reduce working class thinking by creating a larger more affluent middle class. As voting had become more widespread across general populations, then workers unions had grown some organised power in its numbers, and shown a desire to stand up to greed and inequalities, so it posed a possible threat to capitalist power within the workplace. By building up a more comfortable middle class, from an often previously repressed working class, capitalist systems would benefit in two main ways.

Firstly, it benefits by circulating more money through middle classes, creating more demand, more production, more spending and more loans and debt that tie people in to a capitalist economy for the longer term. Secondly though, a middle class that becomes fairly comfortable with its lot is less likely to vote for change or challenge capitalist psychology. In fact, if they were kept fairly distanced and distracted from the extremes of the long term damage that mass production was causing to our planet, and the devastation this could create further down the line, then many of these middle classes might actually vote to support capitalism and really buy into its philosophy, to protect and hopefully increase their own small pots of wealth.

So what is a more complete picture of what capitalist economics and thinking has been doing to our world, what is the full context of the picture? While capitalism has helped improve our innovation and created some more affluent populations in some developed nations, surely such improvements would have taken place and been much more successful just as part of natural human development, under better managed and fairer systems of economic governance, where personal profiteering was outlawed, salaries were more evenly spread, and all excess monies were reinvested in continually improving systems, communities and environments. Where might we be now if these fairer and more sustainable principles had been at the heart of our thinking and governments?

Ok, so a little bit of wishful thinking maybe, but it illustrates a point of comparison, to highlight that perhaps the good that capitalism purports to have been responsible for, could be so much better, if personal profits and wealth were not being constantly drained from the pot. We have looked at the balanced case for capitalism, but what of its more extreme and unbalanced actions and repercussions, when personal greed takes over and the desire for expansion and profit is the only real focus. The extremes of capitalist expansion, in continually looking to raise production and profit margins, is then based on so many unsustainable principles that are all potentially more polluting and damaging to the environment. For a long time, as people have been engrossed in and distracted by the innovative wonder of all this consumerism, and by all of the advertising and entertainments industries, then capitalism has mostly been able to conceal and disguise its destructive elements, at least until the repercussions began to come back on our everyday lives more noticeably.

In this extreme thinking of prioritising only profit, then people and their livelihoods no longer really matter unless they fit into the chain of profit. People are either expendable labour forces, discarded if cheaper labour can be found elsewhere, or they are consumers, who need to be convinced they need ever more products and must be kept consuming. It sounds harsh, but this is how the psychology of capitalism really works, looking at how profit can be increased from every single angle: how can we get cheaper resources; can we use cheaper materials; how can we get labour costs down; can we dispose of waste more cheaply; can we get away with some forms of pollution; how can we expand our consumer base; how can we get our products and logos in peoples minds more; how can we make people loyal to our companies; how much can we get away with charging for items or services; can we control markets better, or create dependencies on our products; can we kill off or buy out our competition. These are just some of the perspectives and questions asked and acted upon in the ruthless world of modern capitalist business, where profit has become the summit of all focus and achievement.

    And so, such thinking has grown throughout our economic and business worlds; ruthless business practice has become admired in the capitalist world, and its best practitioners held aloft as icons to our societies: the all powerful multi-millionaires or billionaires. As the western world abandoned itself to capitalism, so most of the rest of the world followed or were dragged along, and developing countries quickly tried to emulate and compete. Capitalism is primarily based on mass production, mass consumerism and mass consumption, and as it took hold of our human world, while we mostly lost sight of the environmental repercussions, so the damage and pollution has become extensive. Year after year we hear more and more cases of how lands, ecosystems and communities have been decimated or affected by industrialised practises and pollution, and it continues every single day. And now, we have the increase of the repercussions of climate inconsistencies and changes, affecting the balance of our weather patterns, and putting ever more pressure on our environments.

The general thinking of large numbers or our populations has gradually changed and been infected by capitalist greed. People are naturally frightened to lose what they have built up, so they listen to the promises of capitalist governments and vote them in on these questions: how will I profit? How much better off will I be? How much tax can I avoid? Who is offering me the best financial deal? Who will best protect my money and assets? We have become swamped in materialism, and the selfish thinking of greed has become 'normalised', with our voting for government too often asking nothing realistically about the long term future of the planet.

People have been made to become dependant on capitalist politics: many previously public owned services and essential resources have been privatised, as they offer some of the biggest markets and profit opportunities, and, when your water, fuel for energy, and land for food production is all privately owned or controlled by large corporations, to make profits for a small minority, then you truly are being held to ransom. These are the costs of extreme capitalism and the insatiable disease of greed, as it loses sight of humanity and any genuine care for sustainable communities or natural environments. This is the full context and realities of what capitalist governments and economics have actually been achieving, and while we continue to enable it and allow it, this is what continues to go on.

If you are not part of the chain of this extreme commercialism, then you are considered worthless to society: discarded from thought. Populations in poorer countries can starve, often now due to the ongoing climate instabilities that are the repercussions of long term industrial pollution. Sections of society can become ignored and neglected, destitute and homeless, if they are deemed as having nothing to offer capitalism, or if capitalist exploitation has taken the resources of their lands and left political instabilities. All the while the images of capitalist success and riches is being advertised and paraded to the entire world, and if you cannot create capitalist gains legally through your society, then there is a whole other darker world that has grown and expanded under capitalism, with even less humanity and care for other life: the extreme capitalist economies of the black markets.

Chapter 9: The Black Markets of Greed

While all of our societies around the world are trading goods of some form or another, depending on the businesses and the laws of the countries that are trading, then there are usually a whole host of trade laws and standards that must be adhered to, some more checked and monitored than others and with different levels of taxes that must be paid. This all adds to the time and costs of production and trade, usually taking money out of the level of profits that can be made. So if profit is your main priority, then illegal trade and the smuggling of goods has always been an alternative, as there are no standards to adhere to, no taxes to pay and you get to keep all of the profit. Although there are risks if you are caught, it has always proved an attractive proposition to some less scrupulous capitalist entrepreneurs.

Illegal trade and smuggling is just one aspect of what is known as the 'black market', and it has been around since the dawn of more organised societies and their imposition of taxes upon all trade, as not everyone wanted to have to pay taxes to their realm, having done all the hard work of producing and moving goods around. Smuggling could also be a way of avoiding restrictive exchange rates between currencies, and ensuring you received more money for your goods. Or, if items were illegal or scarce in a region, then prices and profits could be driven way up, much increasing the smuggler's incentive. Under particularly oppressive regimes, or leaders who were not particularly respected or liked, then smugglers could become popularised and sometimes notorious, as more people resented the paying of taxes and might look for more ways to avoid having to pay them.

Beyond any romanticised notions of smugglers though, in general, where there are no set standards, no laws, no policing and no safeguarding protocols, then the organisation and running of any type of business enterprise under such conditions, can quickly become dark and dangerous. Those who choose or are forced to trade within the black markets of smuggling and exploitation, are then entering the lawless underbelly of society: a whole different world of criminality. While the criminal element has always existed in societies: smuggling, stealing, abductions, murder, illegal slavery and human trafficking, illegal prostitution; depending upon the laws of the state, then punishments could be relatively quick and severe to discourage the excessive development of crime.

With the onset of industrialisation and the subsequent explosions of trade and capitalist thinking, then the black markets of crime and human exploitation, always opportunistic, have jumped on board and expanded into every corner of society. The black markets of today can involve huge organised crime syndicates, massive arms trades and both private and political wars, massive untaxed revenues and money laundering operations, and sadly, huge increases in murders and human exploitation. Part of the repercussions of selling the thinking and desires of capitalism to the entire world and the rights for everyone to make profits, is that when greed merges with criminality and a lack of fear to consequences, then it will truly stop at nothing to make money and accumulate wealth, power and control.

While they were never presented as the positive merits of capitalism, for obvious reasons, the many and diverse elements of the expansion of organised criminal black markets are very much a direct result of the growth of capitalist thinking. As production and trade exploded across the planet, and people were bombarded with advertising images of rich and lavish lifestyles, for some, that could not see a legal way or opportunity to buy in, then crime was always going to be a possible path to making profit and becoming rich. If you came from a neglected community or a social background where you had nothing, then you might feel you had nothing to lose, and if you kept being shown the affluent lives and exploits of the rich and famous as something we all should look up to, then you have the prefect breeding ground for the psychology of crime and the exploitation of the poor.

Okay, so it is still always a moral decision as to whether or not to enter into crime, but there are certainly many obvious immoralities within the legal exploits of organised capitalism (the use of modern 'slave' labour, the control and restriction of essential resources, the extreme disparities of wealth distribution, the squeezing out of smaller business through undercutting - these are just a few examples). Where profit is the priority, then legal capitalism will always look for a way round, or a loophole, if it can increase profit. Crime just takes this a step further, and if you feel you have nothing to lose, then this can lead to some of the most inhumane and horrific realities that exist in our world today. From street crime wars and murders, to organised crime armies, guns trafficking and wars, to human and child slavery, enforced prostitution and torture; truly the worst elements of human nature, that as a species, we have deviated into.

So what are the elements of these black markets that have been enabled to grow and develop through capitalist systems and ideals; while human nature is obviously responsible for its own actions, extreme capitalist thinking and greed is an aspect and creation of our nature, and these are some of the darker realities of what they have created and how they are challenging the safety and stability of our modern societies. While black markets and illegal trading attempt to avoid government imposed regulations, price controls, rationing laws, taxes and the fixed rates of exchange currencies…, in its totality, the black market is the second biggest economy in the world, and growing. A recently researched estimate, stated that it could account for about 13% of developed nations GDP (gross domestic product) and up to 36% of developing countries GDP. Who really knows, it could even be much higher as nothing is ever officially recorded or declared. So you can appreciate the challenge of its established size and often violent supporting framework, and with absolutely no regulations or subsequent care for consequences, then limiting environmental damage and pollution by illegal trade practices and markets, doesn't even come into consideration.

Illegal market operations usually have two main priorities in mind: making as much money as possible, and not getting caught, and they will usually do anything possible to secure these objectives. The illegal drugs trade across the world has become one of the largest and most organised sections of the black market, setting up links and trafficking routes into almost every major country of the world. It is estimated to generate £500 billion upwards every year (so the true figures could actually be way higher), and with numerous large organised syndicates and cartels established across the globe, producing, manufacturing and distributing the most in-demand illicit drugs to all the major populations of our world, then there is lots of competition, tensions and conflicts. Many of the larger cartels, who have a longer history and have become more established within their home countries, where the drugs are often produced on a large industrial scale, have grown to become influential in policing and politics, to be able to maintain their interests and controls. Some have even built up large arsenals of weapons and sizeable private armies, and so have proved very difficult to stop and to be held accountable.

After the cartels and organisations producing and initially selling the drugs on, there is then all of the 'middlemen' and infrastructures of trafficking, distributing and selling the drugs to the actual consumers. Again this can cause issues and conflict on many levels: border crossings and smuggling, distribution to dealers, local competition and gang rivalry, and the devastating affects of drug addictions, bad reactions to tampered substances and overdoses…, all potentially escalating other forms of crime in these processes, and in the areas of highest consumption. The damaging and costly affects of the illegal drugs trade, and its many direct and indirect crimes, are well established in nearly every major city of the world and many of the smaller towns and cities. Drug crime is an ongoing battle and cost for the entire world's economy, and it often links up with and supports many other elements of the black market and illegal trade.

Illegal arms and weapons trading, sometimes tied in with the illegal drugs trade, is another dangerous element of the black market that can cause or fuel conflict around the world. Although considered one of the less profitable illegal trades, estimated as making between £1-4 billion annually, it is still ranked as the 9th largest criminal market. Arms trading may include: small arms and light weapons, ammunitions and explosives, military ordnance and components, and chemical, biological, radiological and nuclear material for weapons. Supply of weapons is obviously dependant upon demand, so it pays to escalate and maintain conflict if you are in the business of arms trafficking, and with some of the more dangerous substances and terrorist organisations in existence, it is a large scale and expensive commitment for intelligence and security agencies to try to monitor and control.

As well as the illegal drugs trades, there is also a very large black market for the illegal trade of prescription drugs around the world. This can be either manufactured prescription drugs that are being illegally circulated and sold, or the fraudulent selling of fake drugs, which can sometimes be extremely dangerous, due to their unknown composition. The World Health Organisation has stated that around 1 in every 10 medicines fails standards in low and middle income countries, due to falsified or substandard ingredients. Peoples of all ages are dying around the world of treatable diseases and illnesses because the medicines they are given are counterfeit.

The rise of the internet in recent decades, and of online selling and purchasing from all around the world, has opened the floodgates for fake pharmacies, and the general circulation of substandard and counterfeit medicines that can be easily bought online. Others issues also include countries where certain drugs are in low supply or simply not available, so people can be exploited into buying illegal imports at high prices, that may even turn out to be fake. All of this costs lives, and of course, lots of money in trying to control and regulate drugs, as well as stopping illegal supply lines and catching and prosecuting those responsible.

Although these illegal trades are all disturbing, perhaps one of the most distressing and inhumane is that of human trafficking, and all that it can involve. Human trafficking is a kind of modern day slavery business, mostly run by organised crime syndicates and often intertwined with drugs trafficking, especially in the trafficking routes and smuggling techniques. It is estimated as the third most profitable business in illegal trade, possibly bringing in over £30 billion per year, consisting mostly of sex trafficking and slavery, forced labour and involuntary servitude, and migrant trafficking. Many of the more wealthy developed nations actually fuel the demands for forced prostitution, and for slave labour and migrant trafficking into wealthy countries; organised by criminal gangs who can abuse and exploit people, this has been continually on the rise and proved very difficult and expensive to try to counter.

Men, women and children of all ages are kidnapped, forced, coerced and bribed into prostitution and pornography, forced labour and servitude through debt entrapment, and many are lured by the promise of migration to a better life. It has been estimated that around 1,000,000 people are trafficked each year, with many coming from poorer or unstable environments, often originating from Eastern Europe, Southeast Asia and areas of Africa, and then shipped around the world via organised trafficking routes. Another growing and horrific trend linked to human trafficking, is the involuntary harvesting of bodily organs, or the exploitation of the poor to sell their organs for money. All of these realities are truly inhuman, and just goes to show the abhorrent depths that greed has dragged human nature into, just to make money and profit: trafficking, physically and sexually abusing, and even murdering, innocent men, women and children.

Many of the more established crime organisations, perhaps originating from specific illegal markets, then spill into other illegal trades. They also aim over time to set up the cover of many seemingly legitimate businesses, which can then be used to launder money and profits from all their illegal gains. Sales of stolen and counterfeit goods, is another big area of illegal trade around the world, as is software and copyright piracy. Modern cyber crimes of staged frauds, personal details and identity thefts are now stealing billions each year, and the internet has established it own encrypted 'dark web' of sites over the years, to communicate, move monies and even advertise illegal services and sales. One such site, called the 'silk road', operating between 2011 -2013 (when it was shut down), advertised all kinds of illegal drugs and services for sale, using bitcoin payments to protect its profits, which were in the millions. Other similar dark web sites have looked to sell weapons, illegal pornography and even hired killing services.

One of the biggest generators of profit within the black market is actually illegal gambling, which is again often linked with other elements of organised crime and money laundering. There are two main areas of criminality in illegal forms of gambling: one is illegally set up and run casinos, gambling rings and groups, and illegal human and animal fighting, or competitions where unlicensed gambling is the main aim. With all of these there are no taxes paid or controls, other than those enforced by the organised criminals running them, so there is always the danger of fraud, exploitation and violence being involved.

The other area is betting fraud and match or outcome fixing, where inside information may be given on betting, or where organised groups conspire to control the outcome of a competitive betting event in their favour. Both of these offer the potential of making big money by betting and winning through legitimate gambling sites. On-line betting fraud has also increased as the internet has expanded, with cybercriminals attempting to defraud legitimate gambling companies, but also with fraudulent sites attempting to steal personal details and monies. Illegal gambling and gambling addictions are huge problems within society today, often supporting many organised crime groups and their other criminal activities, with hundreds of billions of pounds generated illegally every year.

There are many other illegal trades and markets operating around our world every day. Some of the others that generate the largest sums of profit, and cost our societies the most in trying to police and bring down, are as follows: the illegal theft and smuggling of gas and oil; the illegal dumping of pollutants and hazardous waste; illegal mining, logging and fishing; the illegal wildlife trade and poaching of animals for food or specific body parts; organised piracy and gang thefts. With virtually all of these illegal activities and the numerous cartels, organisations and gangs that run them, there is the ongoing killing, abusing and exploitation of large numbers of people…, and all of this is happening now, as you are reading these words, and every day that we allow this to continue.

As already pointed out, illegal operations usually have two main priorities in mind, making money and not getting caught. There are huge sums of money being made and circulated, all being taken out of the taxable economy, and illegal trade offers no legitimate restrictions and human safeguards. Then there is the ongoing costs of intelligence agencies, policing, wars and conflicts fought with organised crime syndicates, and, of course, the spiralling costs dealing with street crime, drug addictions and fraud. There is the domination of peoples and communities by illegal crime gangs and organisations, and the continual exploitation of peoples, dependant on illegal trade for jobs or forced into servitude. And finally, there is the ongoing damage to our environments via illegal mining, illegal logging, poaching and illegal fishing, and by the illegal dumping of pollutants and dangerous waste…, all to try to avoid costs and to try to fulfil the insatiable desire for profit.

These are just some of the realities of what capitalist thinking and greed psychology have created in our world; they are part of the whole and realistic picture of prioritising making money and profit above care, equality and sustainability. Next, we will go on to look into all of the repercussions and the real challenges that we and our next generations are all having to face up to, now that the issues have become too big to hide any longer or ignore, now that they are really starting to knock on all of our doors and to affect more of our lives directly…

Chapter 10: The Current State and Challenges of the World that we have Created

    You may have realised by now, with the title of this chapter, that everything has been leading up to this point in some way. This chapter is perhaps the most important of the whole book, for what it can offer in awareness; this is 'what we all really need to know', at least to be able to make informed choices about the direction of our future. The previous chapters have been intentionally kept fairly brief, so as not to get weighed down in historical dates and extensive details, or in too many scientific monologues and confusing terminologies. The aim was always to keep things simple, and to offer an understandable trail of how the imbalanced thinking of greed came into being and was able to take such a strong hold of the human mind over time and evolution.

    As all pasts lead to the present; the creative moment where we are alive and the only place that we may truly act from and directly effect and shape the future, then this is the place that requires our greatest attentions and subsequent reactions. The rise and dominance of human greed, to have created and gravitated towards positions of leadership and control, has effected and shaped a truly ludicrous world reality, that we all are now having to face up to: a world where humans are knowingly polluting and destroying the environments that keep them alive; a world where we are literally killing ourselves because of the compulsions of greed.

    The journey from human animal, through our dominant and often violent rise to attempt to control nature and organise productive and profitable societies, has brought us all to the now: the present reality of our world in which we all stand, facing the unknowns of the future, in which we all have at least some power to direct. Looking back at the past, although plagued with violence and inequalities, and gradually manipulated more by the disease of greed (which has, of course, been the main focus of this book's narrative), we have still all come a long way forward as a species, from the often savage animals, just competing to survive.

I look to take nothing away from all of our positive achievements and advancements as a race: from first conquering the use and control of fire, through the innovation and development of tools and the building of organised societies, supported by the progressions of agricultural developments, and onto our modern societies of amazing scientific and material inventions and profound technologies. If an early primitive humanoid were to stand beside one of their modern, well dressed and groomed descendants of today, and to see all the capabilities of their modern world technologies, then I suspect their minds would struggle to cope with the vastness of difference and complexities; they might think that they are looking at a totally different or alien species.

But if we really want to fully understand where we have come from and how we have evolved over the centuries, to appreciate the full picture of where we stand in the present and all the challenges that we now face, then we have to look at the complete picture with honesty and eyes fully opened. We have to pull back the covers, and perhaps to look at the things we might not like or want to see, to appreciate what is operating behind all of our actions, and the less disclosed and less desirable elements of our evolution and developing societies. The disease and imbalance of greed has certainly played a major role in these destructive elements, and established a strong hold on our current psychologies of government and economics throughout the world that we have created.

And this is where we currently stand, at the precipice of the heights of all of our achievements, but with potentially the greatest of falls imaginable ahead of us, if we really do not fundamentally change the destructive and unsustainable actions of our progressive exploits into profit making and greed psychology. The facts and statistics have been out there for many years being pushed around and debated, and there are lots of publications of detailed research and evidence, to help us to really see the impending need to change our unsustainable and damaging systems. Many of these reports, however, can often be so lengthy and scientific in their terminologies, so as to restrict their wider appeal and understanding, and to lose the essence of their simple message: that we all need to take full responsibility and genuinely turn things around. There may also be a feeling for many that our worldwide capitalist economic systems have just become too big to challenge or fundamentally change, and that there are just too many lives and livelihoods tied in to and dependant upon them. All this is has achieved though, is to delay and deny the inevitable, which is just leading us into more damaging repercussions, until we really get the message, en masse, and react accordingly.

What follows, is a run through of all the most serious and challenging issues and problems in our world that we have created for ourselves; the true repercussions of the destructiveness and imbalance of greed, being enabled to gain positions of power and control in our world, on a global scale. They are researched and accredited where appropriate, but they are offered in a straightforward and simple manner, so that everyone can read them and hopefully understand their significance. Beyond this, your reaction is obviously your choice: whether you agree, deny, argue, ignore, or are already aware and committed to change: these things I appreciate are out of my hands. But these are the facts as I have come to see and know them, and I have always considered myself to be fair minded and committed to equality. You can decide for yourselves what these facts mean to you.

In the previous chapter we took a wider look at some of the major elements of our current black markets, and all of the challenges and issues that these are currently posing to our societies, in the way of their human costs, their environmental damages, and their economic drains on public finances, that could, of course, be used for more positive improvements, were our black markets of greed not so extensive, or better still, no longer in existence. If we now go back to look at our currently legalised systems of capitalist economics again, and the many issues created by the extremes of greed psychology, then these are some of the realities of the challenges we are all now facing in our world. Because of the amount of major issues that there are to cover, then they have been split into subsections to try to highlight some of the specifics and importance of each challenge.

Resource Control, Exploitation of Labour and Inequality

Through the large scale controls of resources and their subsequent markets by small amounts of private owners, organised groups and major shareholders, we have facilitated and enabled them to just help themselves to large personal profits. Along with the already inherited wealth of the remaining aristocracies of our world, this has further created an obscenely rich elite class, with powers to buy up more and more resources and to gain even more controls of lands and economies. This creates further divides between an elite rich class controlling resources, production and profit flow, and an often impoverished mass labour force, especially in developing nations, where companies have increasingly set up their industries to exploit the cheap labour, and to avoid the higher salaries and working laws of more developed nations.

Visualcapitalist reported that 1.1% of the total population of the world have 45.8% of the global wealth ($191.6 trillion), while 55% of the population at the bottom end of the scale, share just 1.3 % of the global wealth ($5.5 trillion). You don't need to be an expert mathematician to see that there is an extreme imbalance in wealth distribution here. And for most conscientious humans, there is an obvious morality issue here: what could ever justify enabling someone to have assets of billions and to live in elite luxury (way more then any individual would ever need to live and survive comfortably), while thousands / millions of people in poorer nations are barely able to house and feed themselves from week to week, even though they may be working extremely long hours, often for one of the elite rich's production companies that produces all of this profit and wealth?

This is a commonly repeated reality across the globe today: large impoverished labour forces, often doing all the real work of production over extremely long working weeks, with a tiny minority of elite rich controlling the organisation and flow of finances, and enabled to take most of the generated profit and wealth for themselves. Yes these are examples of the extremes, but they illustrate the current real divisions between the 1% in control and the 55% struggling to survive: genuine extreme disproportional sharing of wealth, legally enabled by capitalist philosophies and economies. This is a direct repercussion of the disease of greed, and its symptomatic lack of feeling or care for the wellbeing of other life.

The majority of peoples on this planet in work are now tied into capitalist systems of extraction, production and commerce;

many livelihoods have become dependant upon often unsustainable industries for their food and survival, and they are often trapped within this cycle. So what happens in the longer term when resources run out, industries move or find cheaper labour elsewhere. Dependencies leave few realistic options, and often entrap people in low wage slave labour, and if industries die out or move, then communities can decay and people can starve or be forced to migrate. If you have no other option, if you have no ability to travel and relocate, if you have families to feed and support, then you can be forced into cheap and unsafe labour, and many larger companies and corporations exploit this around the world just to increase their profits. Even in more affluent societies it is now becoming increasingly common for low level workers on minimum wages to no longer be able to afford their country's basic costs of living, showing that the disproportional sharing of wealth is everywhere.

The UN reported recently that around 28 million people work in forced labour around the world under threat of violence or destitution, with long hours and little pay. A recent Gallup survey, asking 74,000 workers over 121 countries, concluded that 23% of employees had experienced violence or harassment in their workplace of a physical, psychological or sexual nature. The UN has reported that more than 630 million workers worldwide do not earn enough to lift themselves above poverty lines, with 74% of countries actually denying workers the rights to set up and join any trade unions. The International Labour Office listed that approximately 250 million children between 5-14 years, work within sweatshops around the world for low pay, in often dangerous conditions, and for up to 16 hours a day, and millions of these will die due to exploitation, abuse and the unsafe working conditions. Many larger companies simply do not see or care for the human rights of their labour forces, and think only in these simple terms: cheap labour, to make products more cheaply, to maximise profits, to increase the personal profits of their wealthy owners and shareholders, and people, often young women and children, die for this every day. Right now, at the same time that you are reading these very words they are dying, due to unsafe 'slave' labour and abuse, solely for the profit gains of an elite rich.

So with the extremes at either end of these immoral capitalist systems, what about the expanded middle classes who have benefitted to some degree, from more wealth being generated and circulated. Well these often come into too main categories: those in the lower half who are increasingly struggling to cover the costs of living in their country, working longer hours and accumulating more debt…, and those in the top half who are relatively comfortable and often able to keep increasing their wealth and investments, keeping the money flowing through commercialism in full support of capitalism, and often one of the main demographics of voters in general elections, as they look to protect their social positions and incomes, and take the time to vote (where other more disillusioned demographics may not).

What these middle classes mostly have in common is all the wealth of distractions that now goes with more disposable income, and more access to higher levels of credit and borrowing, which now dictate whole lifestyle psychologies. These two elements help to continue funding the consumerism of societies: they keep populations fully embedded within it and invested in it, and they tie people to it for the long term by increasingly long term mortgages, easy credit and extreme debt. Within all of these day to day distractions and occupations that may take up all of your time and thinking: work, mortgages, taxes, bills, borrowing, debt repayments, family, hobbies, entertainments, social media, holidays, weddings, celebrations, funerals…, then you can become fully immersed in this life, and there is increasingly less time to genuinely see and appreciate the wider picture of what is actually happening around the world, with all of its resource depletion to fuel capitalism, its ongoing environment damage, and its extreme poverty and inhumanity.

Distraction of populations has long been the main cover to concealing the darker and more destructive elements of capitalism, and to enabling a wealthy elite to remain in control. The majority of the poor and exploited labour forces are often far too busy just working and trying to feed and house themselves and their families from week to week, while the middle classes are so engrossed in their more affluent lifestyles, and its many entertainments and self-imposed stresses, that little time is left to look deeper, or if they do, to genuinely and fundamentally change the things that their lifestyles are now so dependant upon. For most people, especially those engrossed in middle class lifestyles and all of its material follies, entertainments and stresses, then it is not until trouble actually physically knocks on your door, or begins to threaten your livelihood, that you actually look up and take notice, and seriously begin to think about what really needs to change.

Throughout all of these modern lifestyles under capitalist economies, two things are repeatedly common in populations throughout the world and across most class divisions, save the wealthy elite: high levels of stress and increasing mental illness, and high levels of poverty or debt: the two nearly always being closely connected. HSE statistics in the UK reported upward trends in work related ill health, with around half of the 1.8 million reported cases in 2022/23, being attributed to stress, depression and anxiety. The World Economic Forum reported in 2020 that according to the Global Workplace Report, 43% of respondents in over 100 countries claimed to be experiencing stress, with the highest being 57% in the USA and Canada. The WorldBank.org listed that the number of poor below the poverty level of $2.15 per day (2017 PPP - purchasing power parities across different country's economies) was 689 million in March 2024, and for the poverty level of $6.85, it was 3589 million. In March 2024, the Money Charity organisation shared the statistics that people in the UK owed over £1,800 billion in debt, while the International Monetary Fund declared the rise of Global debt to have reached $226 trillion by 2020.

Okay, so just a few statistics to illustrate the points while populations are continually on the rise; there are very high levels of poverty around the world, peoples are increasingly stressed and worried about debt and instabilities, and figures of worldwide debt are immense. But where does all this credit come from, and who is all the debt owed to, who is profiting from all of this lending and reclaimed interest? The simple answer is, capitalist banks and credit and finance companies mainly, ever increasing their controls of finance and ever increasing the profits of the elite rich. Although lending and repayment agreements have existed between countries and nations for many years, managed by their government economies and banking systems, with the expansions of capitalism, then commercial banks looked to exploit any potential market, actively seeking ways to reach new businesses and countries to lend to, with healthy interest rates, high potential profits, and good collateral safeguards if available.

With the controls on oil supplies under OPEC (The Organisation of the Petroleum Exporting Countries - an organised and elite group of representatives, for the major oil producing countries), then the prices of oil were hugely increased in the early 1970's. This then hit newly developing countries very hard as they were trying to compete and improve their industries and economies, which needed large amounts of oil to fuel their developments. Many commercial western banks then quickly seized the potential to step in and to set up lending agreements to fund developments and help with the pressures of the oil price increases. This also gave them a foot in the door to the wider economies and resources of many of these countries, to create more financial ties, and to encourage more outside business investments.

    Lots of borrowed finance then began to flow into developing nations from the commercial banks and loan companies, and this was happening alongside further exploitation, as large corporate companies targeted the resources and cheap labour forces of developing nations: lending monies, supporting political regimes in power, setting up mining operations, businesses and industries, and enabling countries to fall into further debt by taking most of the wealth back out of the countries, and only supporting the rich elites in control. With changes in economic policies, inflation and interest rates over the years, and due to sometimes volatile markets, then many of the developing countries had debts and accrued interest that they simply could not pay back, and this was damaging their economies and causing further issues of poverty. Arguments toed and froed, that it was the fault of these countries for borrowing beyond their means, or that the commercial banks were to blame for irresponsible lending; either way, throughout this period, the people and resources of these developing countries were being exploited, and capitalist greed was making its profits.

    The consumption and use of fossil fuels in our world has been increasing almost exponentially since the rapid expansions of its industrial uses began in the 1800's. Although coal use has been falling in many parts of the world recently, due to it being harder to extract cost-effectively as supplies drain, oil and gas use has picked up the slack and has grown rapidly. So much of our world and its economies now rely on their use for production, for transport and for domestic energy; our populations have become massively dependant upon it for many of the essentials of our modern lifestyles. The CU200 (Carbon underground 200) compiled by the FFI (Fossil Free Indexes), identifies the top 200 coal, oil and gas companies in our world; between them, they own and control about 98% of proven reserves. Of these, the vast majority are privately owned businesses with shareholders, prioritising profits, with only a few government backed institutions holding any large stakes. When the profits are published by these firms in control of our resources, often huge profits, then it doesn't take a genius to realise that we are often being held to ransom in the prices that are being controlled and charged. And this private control, that prioritises personal profiteering to fund elitist wealth, is also why the use of fossil fuels is being forced to continue and to maintain our dependence.

The control of essential resources in our world by private enterprises, to control markets and prices and generate personal profits, has then expanded outwards with capitalist thinking to try to gain a hold on more and more of the mass public industries, that offer guaranteed long term profits due to unquestionable need and demand. Control of water services and public transport networks by private companies has increased significantly around the world, sometimes taking over complete systems, and sometimes being subcontracted to run particular aspects and services. If these are taken over from previous public controls, then often there are public subsidies from government taxes to support these companies, under the promises of increased investments to improve running and efficiency. But repeatedly the realities are in the longer terms that private companies focused on profit, gradually push up prices and cut back and undermine the services, by taking out vast sums of money each year via personal profiting, inflated management salaries and shareholder dividends…, all monies that could help reduce prices for the public and be continually reinvested into improving the service. Some private companies have then used public subsides and incurred debts, while still taking out personal profits each year, and then later handed the services and its debts back to governments, if financial gains were becoming more challenging.

  As just one example of a practice that has been common in the world of capitalist thinking, here is an outline of a report made by the Independent in 2017, regarding water privatisation in England. In the late 1980's most of the publicly-owned water companies (built with public monies) were sold off by the then government, for around £7.6 billion, with the government solely absorbing the £5 billion of the sectors existing debt, hence giving the new private owners a debt free business. These water companies had been underfunded by government for some time, who had also restricted their ability to borrow, so improvements were needed in services and water quality across the country. This could have been done with new government controlled investment, keeping the industry non-profit making and focusing entirely on reinvestment, but instead private companies were given the reigns and the powers to take out profits.

  Water services were first improved to fall in line with European standards, and some money was invested to improve water qualities, but not nearly as much as was needed long term, especially to maintain these improvements. After just three decades of private management, then over 70 % of the shareholder's ownership lay with external international investors, many of which were based in tax havens, taking monies out of the country. Most water supplies became metered, partly to reduce wastage, but mostly to improve companies incomes, as prices of water services rose by 40%. New investment was often financed by borrowing rather than shareholder investments, and over the decades, the new private owners had managed to build up a debt of over £46 billion between them (by 2016). Over a quarter of what the public were then paying on their bills was going towards debt interest and paying out dividends to shareholders (mostly outside of the country). In the ten years leading up to 2016, the private companies made a combined post-tax profit of £18.8 billion, of which just over £18 billion was paid out in dividends to shareholders…, all money that could have gone back into improving the system. Three companies actually paid out more money to shareholders than the actual total of their pre-tax profits.

Now some of the private companies are saying they are struggling with the repayments of the debt that they have created while managing these water companies, especially with interest rate rises. While more private and shareholder reinvestment is finally being proposed, it will undoubtedly not be enough (too little and too late), and shareholders are unwilling to put money back into their companies if the business is no longer profitable for them. So the more likely scenario is that the shareholders and company owners move on (with the billions they have taken out over the years), and the company is taken back into public ownership, with all of its debts and the costs of needed improvements going back into the hands of government, or more accurately, in the hands of the bill payers and tax payers: the general public, the original builders and owners of the water systems.

A more lengthy example perhaps but one that shows what greed has genuinely been doing to many of our services around the world over recent decades. Many of us have been being distracted and placated with the right words and promises of our capitalist governments and businesses when pushing through privatisation; we have been being given some improvements, some signs of initial investment (often subsidised with public monies), but then services are often economised (reduced) and prices are increased. In reality then, when profit is prioritised, the reinvestments become the minimums agreed (where services can become run down and failing over time), and profits taken out by owners and shareholders become maximised.

When people are forced to be dependant upon private companies for the provisions of their essential resources, then if there are no effective safeguards, they can begin to be held to ransom, and prices start to be aimed at how much can be charged, rather than the fair worth of a service or item; 'how much can we get away with and increase profit margins by?'. This pressure of extreme capitalism just keeps pushing prices and profits up, in a boom and bust scenario, until eventually there is a crash; the elite wealthy tend to protect their gains and move on, while the general populations are left to pay the price and have to live with the consequences. All of these issues and pressures on our societies, stem from resource controls: if we allow small groups of individuals, running private companies for personal profits to have legal control of the majority of our resources, then we are often enabling greed to take control, and for labour forces and people to be exploited. This is a proven reality of our current capitalist world, and we are all having to face the consequences, and pay the price, of allowing it to continue.

Advertising Pressure and Manipulation

Another rapidly expanded industry of commercialism that has grown to reach into and impose itself upon every area of our lives, is that of marketing and advertising. Since the beginning of trade there have been simple forms of advertising in play: the attractive displaying of one's goods, the calling out within the market, the talking up of your produce and even the early painting of murals, the carving of signs and the use of flags to attract attention. An ad was found in Egypt from as far back as 3000 BCE, written on papyrus, that was made by a slaveholder trying to find a runaway slave, but also promoting their weaving shop. So advertising has had a long presence in human society, and makes good sense if you are earning a living from selling goods.

Advertising moved on with the advent of the printing press in the mid 15th century, and the first newspaper advert was printed in the US around the start of the 18th century. Billboards came more into use and signs and posters were created for displays outside shops, all starting to develop the thinking of how to capture peoples' attentions and inflate their desires. Then leaflet printing and mailing became a popular technique for a while, as companies developed and started to actually look to spend money on new ways to advertise and to reach out to people.

As the inventions of radio and then television began to find their ways more and more in to the homes of the general public through the 20th century, then the flood gates really started to open for advertising and the growth and expansion of advertising companies, with more targeting and persuasive psychologies. Companies started spending huge budgets on radio and tv advertising and the developments of characters and logos for their brands for the long term, that could really be easily recognised and imprinted within people's minds. This progressed even further with the creation and rapid expansion of the internet and of social media over the last few decades, where now advertisers could track and use personal data to directly target products to individuals, and paid 'influencers' with millions of online followers could be used to shamelessly sell products and brands.

With the new technologies of radio, tv and then the internet, that could reach huge worldwide audiences of millions, then the commercial focus on advertising really exploded. The early psychology of advertising, in how to attract attention and to make your products seem the most desirable, was already there as a foundation. Now, with all the time and money being poured into it, advertising psychology took a real turn, and, in many elements, directed by greed and its desire for profits, it started to develop its own 'dark arts' in how to invade people's minds and manipulatively direct their thinking towards specific brands and products, and general excessive consumerism.

Modern commercial advertising now employs many techniques of both brainwashing and subliminal implanting, constantly looking to compete for attention and bombard our minds with pressure. It has become a huge area of social influence and control for consumer enterprises and their capitalist psychologies. Now this may sound extreme to some, as advertising has tried to be clever and many of us may just accept it as being there as just part of modern day society. When we take a look a little deeper, however, then you can begin to see the darker elements of manipulation that are behind its directives, and the extremities that greed has really taken this too; all to drive consumerism forwards within our minds, and ultimately, to increase the profits and personal wealth of those in control.

Firstly, under capitalist psychologies, then people are thought of and even referred to, as consumers or customer bases.

Early techniques at capturing consumers attention began quite simple and obvious: billboards, large signs, written ads, all gradually becoming more elaborate as they competed for your attentions. With the spread of radio and TV and more time and money invested, then advertising specialists developed their services, and thinking delved deeper into what made people tick, what grabbed their attention or triggered a reaction and emotional response. If you could get into peoples minds and establish a connection and foothold, then you could possibly grow this and refer back to this through repeated sensory recalls. Advertising companies knew this and researched this, and so a whole host of new, less obvious techniques began to branch out and grow, all competing for our mind space and their triggers for consuming.

These new techniques began with more catchy slogans and word play (how many of you can still remember some of these from the adverts of your own childhood, or visualise the images and products?). There were also more catchy tunes being written to specifically get us to hold them and 'sing' along in our heads, and these, along with the slogans, were being repeatedly pushed out through all media available, as part of planned advertising campaigns, seeking to help to imbed them in our minds and to build new commercial empires. Tunes and slogans worked alongside brand logos, as companies began to spend millions on designing advertising strategies and establishing their logos within all society (again we could probably all recognise and recall a vast number of these, that have been their throughout our lives and now are common across the globe).

The psychology of how to get into people's minds and make them think and connect, or how to trigger an emotional response and connect this with a product, all continued to be intentionally developed and to branch out: comforting ads were looked at (in the pleasures of foods and luxury items), funny and comical ads or completely zany off the wall ads (creating things that would shock or make an impact, that people might talk about, imitate and hold in their minds), progressive series of ads (that people might follow and invest in), and adds that would either pull on the heart strings or raise fear and insecurity about issues, only to then offer the solution in the offered services or goods (mortgage lenders, credit, insurance, home security, health etc..). Advertisers also started to seek out and employ the services of celebrities and sports personalities, and to use the most popular songs of the time to endorse and become connected to their products; they have been literally paying millions for the famous and well known to advertise all manor of products, in the knowledge that people will buy them, purely due to the endorsements of their favourite celebrities.

    Advertising would also start to target the times of day, depending on the type of audience who might be listening or watching, or the time of year, season or holiday, when certain ads might increase and flood the media, all competing for your mind space and business. It would also look at different age groups and demographics, and how best to tap the markets of children, youths, the middle aged and the elderly, targeting each in different well researched ways with the products they are most likely to buy. Advertising is everywhere in the backgrounds of our lives: in papers, magazines, posters, hoardings, busses and vehicles, billboards and neon lights…, and it is constantly being thrown at us daily from every angle, through radio and tv, internet and social media, repeating its images and message over and over.

    Subliminal advertising, as another tactic that is used, has long been a subject of debate because its aim is direct manipulation of the minds and actions of people, below their conscious radar. Because of this more deceitful approach, then advertising companies that use it will rarely disclose this openly, and so professional organisations have been directed to scrutinise its possible use; as its messaging is mostly hidden and concealed though, then it can be very hard to detect and prove. Subliminal advertising techniques are like subtle forms of hypnosis, in that they try to influence the actions of potential customers by tapping subconscious programming and responses: hidden symbolisms, images, sounds or words that are often added into other media and disguised to the conscious eye, flashed at speeds that are not immediately detectable, or hidden in sensory manipulation of colour, lighting, sound and visual effects.

It is no coincidence, in a consumer dominated world and economy, that the internet has been expanded so rapidly, and that even in the poorest of nations, devices and internet access have been made readily available, due to the huge profit markets they can enable access to. On the one hand it is a great advance in communication and information sharing that can benefit us all, but would the companies making the devices have sought to reach every nation so quickly and to make their technologies so readily available, were the darker potentials of the internet not so potentially profitable and powerful at reaching into our minds?

The internet is disproportionally being used as a data gathering tool and window for advertising, influencing and commerce. For a longtime, without most of us even knowing, data was being secretly collected and analysed for algorithms to collate, and then to direct back at us the most likely ranges of products that we might look to consume. Individually our habits and searches are being recorded, and then images and links being sent back to us for the very things we might have been recently searching for, or they would start to appear within the scrolls of our social media, that are constantly being tailored to the type of things we have shown that we like to watch and search for, through our personal internet usage.

Social media and advertising on the internet have become increasingly linked over time, ever pushing their values up, with huge sums being paid out collectively by advertising to use the social media platforms and data. Whenever you sign up to a site, especially a commercial selling site, you are often giving them personal details such as phone number and email, and unless you read through and are able to opt out, then you will be added to automated lists to be regularly hit with text and email prompts for buying goods, or for visiting sites with 'sales' promotions. They all want and are competing for your money and business, often increasing the links they send around monthly pay times, or targeting ads for products that you have searched for or purchased previously.

If you think people are not being entranced and brainwashed by addictions to the internet and its social medias and gaming worlds, then try to think back to how many times recently you have seen people gathered together in a social situation, only to nearly all be glued to their individual phones. People now often cannot sit with themselves without reaching for their phone to scroll; the modern day zombies of the social / commercial world, are data eaters, locked to the window of their phones and being directed in so many aspects of their thinking without even knowing or realising it. This is an observation rather than a judgement, as technology is having such a profound effect on people's lives and attentions, and this is the main intention behind most of its designs and excessive distribution and unrelenting upgrading.

People are mostly only doing what they are repeatedly being encouraged and told to do, through advertising and market flooding; if the internet and mobile phones had not been mass produced, advertised and handed out, along with the rapid development of internet providers and endless apps, then much fewer of us would be using them. You can see how quickly things are produced and marketed when profits are to be made. Imagine if we only showed the same urgencies and speeds with sustainable technologies, to implement and establish them across the globe, for all nations. We have proved that it can be done with mobile phones and their networks; it is just about what our urgent priorities are aimed at, and who has the controls and is pushing the agendas.

With all the pressures and tactics of advertising, those more susceptible can genuinely be drawn in and taken over by consumerism; a kind of variant disease of the mind, produced by the overwhelming influences of the extreme original greed that is pushing all advertising and consumer desire. With easily enabled credit, then via gambling or obsessive consumerism, it can be easy in today's world for individuals to build up large debts with high interest rates, that those in debt may then not be able to repay. Lives can be ruined and families torn apart, and sadly today increasing numbers of people are taking their own lives due to debt pressures. The systematic pressures of modern intrusive advertising, reaching into our minds from every direction, often plays a big role in the obsessions that drive people into debt. A recent survey in the UK, commissioned by their NHS, found that in just one year, over 420,000 people with problem debts had considered suicide, with more than 100,000 actually attempting to take their own lives..., and this is just for one country over one year.

Unsustainable Economics and Social Instabilities:

When societies and their economies are run by mostly unsustainable forms of production and commercialism, and capitalist thinking governments are mostly focused on the more wealthy areas of their society, then there will always be underlying instabilities in their long term futures. Two things that can escalate any social instabilities further are, huge disparities and divides between rich and poor sections of society, and a lack of investment and support for the poorer communities. When you add all of these things together, then there are lots of resulting social issues, instabilities and problems in the making.

With the constant increase in populations around the world, then the poorer sections of society are ever expanding. In many poorer developing nations this can mean bigger and bigger pressures on the resources to survive, and a growing population of people living in makeshift slums and shanti towns, as they flock to highly populated city areas in the hope of work and a means to support themselves. These neglected sections of society, sometimes deemed as illegal in certain countries, often have unsafe dwellings built with scrap materials, little access to clean water and healthcare, poor or no sanitation, high levels of sickness and disease, little means of education for the children, and high levels of unemployment, crime and drug use.

In 2020 the UN released statistics that nearly 1.1 billion people (over one eighth of our entire population) were living in slums or slum-like conditions, and they predicted on current trends, that by 2050 up to 2 billion more may be pushed into living in such conditions. Of this total number, then 85% of these people were concentrated in three main regions of the world: Central and Southern Asia, East and South-East Asia and Sub-Saharan Africa. While there are many positive initiatives from the peoples living within slums to try to improve their living conditions, and they do have their own micro economies, the fact remains that they are severely neglected sections of society with many ongoing instabilities, and the situations are mostly getting worse, due to the pressures of ever rising populations.

Unsustainable industries that deplete local resources for production, or create temporary dependencies for jobs and the local economies of communities, after eventually moving on, often leave damaged environments behind and communities struggling for ways to support themselves. The social instabilities of neglected communities are certainly not restricted to poorer developing regions and countries however, there are large numbers of poorer sections of society throughout the western world and its many cities, again with poor living conditions and high levels of unemployment, drug use and crime. As costs of living have increased in many western societies, often driven by the controls of elite corporations over our essential resources, as they strive to maintain their high profits at the people's expense, then the large scale collapse of smaller businesses, bankruptcy, home repossession and homelessness, have all been on the rise, further escalating fears and social instabilities.

Since the Covid-19 pandemic between 2019 and 2022, and with all of the financial pressures this caused with reduced transports and trade, there have been some temporary subsidies and safeguards in place within some countries, to try to protect businesses and homeowners. But with these ending and many other pressures on the costs of living, such as mass inflation and interest rate rises, increased fuel costs, over priced housing and rent markets…, then more and more people are struggling to cover their living costs. Many of these issues, whilst being triggered by different world events, are the early repercussions of having unsustainable capitalist economic models; the get rich quick schemes of over use of resources, over production of products, exploitation of labour and continually forced price rises to maintain or increase profits. The thinking in most of these models is never for long term stability, it is about making money now, for personal profit and elite lifestyles, that many in the business world, infected with greed psychologies, have come to believe they are entitled to.

    But as resources are depleted and populations rise, then fears and instabilities also rise within all societies, and pressures can just continue to increase until they reach breaking point. If there has been little contingency for this in long term planning, because profit has been the main economic point of focus and switches to sustainability have been held back and minimised, then societal structures eventually start to break down and collapse. The desperations of migrations start to increase exponentially as poverty can quickly fall into mass famine, and people are forced to move to seek a living elsewhere, as they may otherwise die. If supply chains are affected for essential food and resources, then all of these dependencies we have created through mass production and profit psychologies, means there are very few capabilities left for the self-sufficiency of mass populations. Economic collapse can then lead to demonstrations, fear, panic, rioting and looting, as survival instincts kick in and override social laws and civilities, especially for the sections of society most under threat.

    It can all can sound very apocalyptic, or is this just another pressure of fear mongering; but these issues and realities are all already there within our societies on smaller escalating scales. Perhaps, in part, this is what has driven all of the entertainments media's focus and fascination with apocalyptic futures, simply because when you look at and weigh up all the facts and evidence, we are actual heading in that possibly apocalyptic direction. While there are many and varied contributing elements to societal instabilities and breakdowns, two of the most prominent are the extreme unsustainable production methods of profit driven economies, that care little for the environment and poorer mass populations, and, the huge disparities in wealth distribution, that have created such a wide divide between a small elite controlling rich population, and a continually expanding massive poorer population, facing increasing living pressures and desperation.

Modern Wars and Terrorism

Instabilities, threats of war and conflicts, have never really left human societies throughout their entire history and development. In our modern age, while the majority of our nations are now fairly well established and have good trade agreements and treaties between them, there are still many instabilities and conflicts being fought around the world. According to UN statistics in 2022, up to 2 billion people were living in conflict affected areas in our world, with an estimated 84 million people being forcibly displaced due to conflict, violence and human rights violations. There are 32 countries currently with active wars, being a mix of disputes between nations, border wars, civil wars, terrorist insurgences, drug wars, gang wars and ethnic violence. The largest of these by casualties (in the thousands) are: Ukraine (Russian / Ukrainian war), Palestine (Israel/ Palestine war), Myanmar (Civil War), Sudan (Terrorist Insurgency), Nigeria (Terrorist Insurgency), Somalia (Civil War), Burkina Faso (Terrorist Insurgency), Mexico (Drug War), Syria (Civil War)…, and the list goes on.

As we have looked at in previous chapters, human beings have an extensive history of wars and conflict, and even now, with all of the social progressions that have taken place over the centuries, fear and insecurity still dominates much of our thinking when it comes to the possible intentions of other nations. There are many social instabilities within our societies: religious and ethnic conflicts, political and economic disputes, and historic enmities that are still driving nations into war. As we still fail to be able to overcome our fears and rivalries, and to realise the huge potentials of us all working together and supporting each other as one race, then the maintenance of large armies and the development and stock piling of weapons is still one of the main investments of every major country in our modern world.

Military spending across the world totalled around 2.44 trillion in 2023, that's money spent in just one year on the maintenance of armies, navies and air forces, arms and weapons production, maintenance and purchases, equipment and facilities, military operations in action, and weapons and technology development. The Stockholm International Peace Research Institute (SIPRI) published the military spending figures for our major countries for 2023 as follows (ranked in order of the top 10): USA $916bn (37% of global military spending), China $296bn (12% of global total), Russia $109bn, India $83.6bn, Saudi Arabia $75.8bn, UK $74.9bn, Germany $66.8bn, Ukraine $64.8bn, France $61.3bn and Japan $50.2bn. Huge annual sums of money for what many countries describe as national defence, but with all of these trained armies and destructive weapons being constantly maintained and developed, then there will always be wars and conflicts in our world, until we can truly progress beyond our deeper fears and insecurities and their violent and primitive nature.

Many of the dangers today lie in insurgencies and terrorism, and in the development of ever more destructive weapons, that in the wrong hands could be unleashed on mass civilian populations. Millions is spent on intelligence agencies across the globe each year, to study, research and track the possible threats of terrorism, in the hope of stopping further human casualties and disasters. Nuclear, chemical and biological weapons could potentially wipe out millions, and seriously damage environments for the long term; if we choose to look down these avenues of weapons research, and direct and fund the developments of such madness, then someone, somewhere, may end up using one of them.

There are numerous listed organised terrorist groups in existence around the world today. WorldData reported that the most widespread are, the Taliban, Islamic state, Boko Haram and Al-Shabaab, and between them, over the period of 2013-2017, they carried out around 13,600 attacks and killed 72,519 people. The sad reality of our current world is that most of our major nations are all on constant alert and lookout for terrorist activities and possible attacks, with innocent civilians regularly being the targets and victims. And this is just another peripheral pressure and threat, that can add to the insecurities and instabilities of our modern societies.

Waste and Pollution

The waste and pollution that we generate as a species has always been a challenge for our societies to manage, especially as concentrated populations have grown in expanding towns and cities. Managing the human waste of large populations has prompted the developments of sewerage systems and sanitation to progress, otherwise disease and ill health can become big threats and issues to larger societies. Historically though, in general, items were made to last and to be repaired if they could be, and food was more directly organic and rarely wasted if possible; ever increasing profit margins had not yet become a top priority in our psychology, which was still based more on practicality and survival during the earlier developments of our growing societies.

With the expansions of industrialisation, however, and the rapid developments of capitalist processes of mass extraction, production and commercialism, driven to extremes by the imbalances of greed, then waste production has exploded across the entire globe. The wastes and pollutions produced in material extractions, transportation and manufacturing have been continually increasing, and the overproduction of cheaper, shorter life goods and of mass varieties of food, now contributes to waste and pollution statistics that are truly staggering; we are running out of places to hide and bury this ridiculous amount of waste, and it is literally starting to spill back on us and poison us and our natural environments. Waste and pollution are two of the biggest growing, life threatening problems that we now face as a species; issues that we are aware of and that are completely of our own making, so we have complete control of how we react and deal with them. Yet, as the capitalist thinking of greed is still directing so many of our governments and economies, then waste and pollution still just continue to increase and to literally kill millions of people every year.

Using recent statista, UN and The World Bank statistics to elaborate: we are currently producing over 2.1 billion metric tons of municipal solid waste every year (if this were all put on average size waste trucks, then end to end, they would go around the world approximately 24 times), and at current rates, this is predicted to increase by over 70% to around 3.8 billion tons by 2050. This waste has been being dealt with in a number of ways:

open site dumping (literally just transported and dumped in large open designated areas), landfill (dumped in areas and buried), incineration (burning, which can add to air pollution and still leave ash waste), specialist hazardous waste treatment and storage (regulated treatments and sealed storage sites), littering and illegal waste dumping (usually directly into the environment), recycling and repurposing (turning waste into new products or reusing it for a different purpose), and organic waste treatment (using organic waste for composting and anaerobic digestion, that produces biogas and nutrient rich digestate for soil conditioning). Over 90% of waste in low income countries is currently dumped openly or burned.

Of the 2.1 billion tons of waste we create every year, around 50% of this is food waste, which contributes to about 10% of global greenhouse gas emissions. Just think on this for a minute: in a world with huge growing populations, and high numbers of people in poverty who often struggle to feed themselves and their families, up to 40% of the food we produce worldwide is wasted, mainly due to commercial models that prioritise mass production, diversity and competition, focused mainly on profit margins. Also largely responsible, due to the indoctrinated consumer driven psychologies that encourage people to buy much more than they actually need to eat in wealthier countries, is domestic greed, that leads to excessive domestic waste in wealthier countries. Agricultural food production also accounts for nearly 70% of the worlds water usage, so due to the vast amounts of food waste and industrial overproduction, then huge quantities of water are also being wasted each year, which could be used more directly by populations struggling for usable water.

We currently produce over 400 million tons of plastic waste every year around the world, with 36% of this being just for packaging, 85% of which goes into landfill. About 98% of single use plastics that cannot be recycled, are made from fossil fuels. Around 11 million tons of plastic waste end up in our oceans each year, with an estimated 171 trillion pieces of plastic now in our world's oceans, killing fish and sea animals, and damaging aquatic environments. Only around 9% of plastic waste is being recycled, so 91% is pure waste, and much of the recycled plastic is made into other plastic items that then later become waste items themselves. Recycling initiatives are certainly increasing and creating new industries, but they barely make a real impact on waste and can do nothing for the statistics on single-use plastics. Just in the last two decades, where we have become more aware and begun recycling initiates, plastic production worldwide has still doubled.

Another growing type of classified waste is electronic waste, or E-waste: recorded at around 62 million metric tons for the year 2022, it is predicted to grow by over 30% in the next decade, up to 82 million tons by 2030. E-waste covers the waste of types of electronic items and technologies, and with these items being flooded onto the markets over recent decades, with consumer strategies of cheaper production methods and constant upgrades, then their waste levels are on a continual rise. Some of these items contain hazardous materials such as lead, mercury and cadmium, that are harmful to both the environment and to humans, if they leak into soils and water sources.

Only around 20% of E-waste is currently recycled properly each year, even though there are often valuable metals that can be extracted and reused. An estimated 48 million tons are collected informally, with 29% of this being disposed of in general waste (open dumps and landfill). Much of it, 75-80%, is shipped to poorer countries in Africa and Asia, where waste management systems are cheaper and less regulated, and populations are less protected from pollution, and this, unfortunately, is a common practice of the global waste trade. The waste trade is another mass industry in itself, and so if profits can be made and corners can be cut to help to increase these profits, then often the cheapest and potentially more environmentally damaging methods of disposal will be prioritised.

All of these types of waste, directly or indirectly, can seriously affect environments and levels of air and water pollution. Some of the other major types of waste are: human waste and domestic product waste (sewerage - sometimes treated but often raw, and all chemical domestic product waste), industrial waste (from fossil fuel use, manufacturing processes, petroleum industries, power plants and chemical plants), agricultural wastes (livestock wastes, pesticides, methane pollution, waste harvested materials), construction and demolition wastes (concrete, treated wood, asbestos, packaging, chemicals, and other building materials not recycled), mining wastes (land damage, wash off, refining wastes, harmful gases), excess commercial wastes (from outdated items, overproduction, falls in demand, and expired or 'unpresentable' foods), and of course, the highly dangerous radioactive wastes from mining and nuclear power production.

Taking all of these types of waste into account, we will now have a look at some of the most prominent and damaging pollution statistics that relate the dangerous imbalances and instabilities now facing our world. Despite lots of initiates to improve sanitation globally, over half the population of the world still use sanitation services that do not treat human waste. In developing countries, about 14 billion litres of untreated faecally contaminated wastewater is created each day (approximately 5,600 Olympic sized swimming pools), and most of this flows into watercourses, rivers and oceans. All of this is contributing to high levels of sickness and disease in these areas, and to aquatic environmental damage. Even in more developed western nations, incidents of sewerage spills can be common as water sanitation systems have not been reinvested in and updated over the years: the BBC reported that in the UK, sewerage spills more than doubled in 2023 from the previous year, and according to the UK Environment Agency, there were 3.6 million hours of spills in that year, when inadequate water systems were either overrun or left damaged and leaking.

Chemical contaminations of oceans can come from several sources of human waste. There is industrial waste that is washed out into watercourses, agricultural run off from farms, and also phosphates from domestic products that are treated in sewerage works, but still affect and reduce biodiversity. While the wastewater from industries is required to be monitored and treated in most developed countries, this has not always been the case, and many spillages and illegal dumpings do still happen, although not always detected and flagged. In developing nations, then spillages and discharges of pollutants into water bodies is less managed, and wastes can often be untreated.

The International Water Association reported in 2018 that around 80% of all industrial wastewater was discharged into water channels and could create pollution and threat to human and aquatic life. The UN Water reported in 2017 that approximately 70% of wastewater is treated in high-income countries, 38% in upper-middle, 28% in lower-middle and only 8% in low-income countries. This equates to approximately 80% of global waste water being discharged without treatment. According to a study published by The Lancet several years ago, there were around 1.8 million deaths caused by water pollution in the year 2015, and human pollution as a whole, is responsible for around 9 million premature human deaths every year.

Perhaps one of the most talked about types of pollution that we produce in the world, and the most damaging and deadly, is air pollution. The balance of greenhouse gasses in our planets atmosphere are vitally important for maintaining more consistent temperatures, climate cycles and weather patterns; they trap in heat from the Sun, which keeps it closer to the Earth's surface, and this helps to regulate temperatures and allow eco-systems to remain stable and flourish. If the balance of the gases are altered for any reason, then temperature levels can change, and climate and weather patterns can alter and become unstable. All our major planetary eco-systems and human agricultural cycles depend on balanced weather patterns and consistent temperatures. Since the beginning of human industrialisation and the subsequent continued increase of the burning of fossil fuels and of industrialised farming, both of which release greenhouse gases into the atmosphere, then the balance of gases in our atmosphere has begun to noticeable change.

The main ways we are polluting the atmosphere, mainly due to industrial excesses of production, are apparent in several ways. Firstly, there have been huge increases in carbon dioxide (CO_2) emissions, that can stay in the atmosphere for hundreds or even thousands of years, mainly produced from the burning of coal, oil, gas, wood and solid waste. Then there are increasing methane gas emissions (CH_4) that can hang around for up to 12 years, produced from burning natural gas, degrading landfill, petroleum industries, and livestock digestive systems. There are also increasing Nitrous oxide (N_2O) emissions that can stay around for over a century, produced from fertiliser, manure and livestock, as well as from burning fuel and agricultural residues. And also there are several other fluorinated gases being released as pollutants, lasting from hundreds to thousands of years, used in manufacturing and as refrigerants and solvents. Vehicle combustion engines are a big polluter, as well as electricity production, and anything else that burns fossil fuels. Currently, there are about twenty countries responsible for more than three-quarters of the total world emissions, including the USA (the biggest polluter), China, Russia, Brazil, Indonesia, Germany, India and UK, in order of the most cumulative emissions.

It takes vast amounts of gases to have an impact on the balance of our atmosphere, but the increase and spread of industrialised practices for commercialism has been increasingly polluting the atmosphere for many decades now. Carbon dioxide is the primary greenhouse gas, with three quarters of human pollution emissions being CO_2, although climate changes are also affecting CO_2 emissions in other areas of our planet's geology. By the 1980's the proofs of climate change due to pollution were starting to become apparent, and the governments and general populations were being warned of the dangers of continuing with these immense levels of industrial pollution. In the 250 years leading up to 1990 human pollution of CO_2 had gone from virtually unnoticeable to the atmosphere, to reach a total of about 785 billion extra metric tons. After these warnings about pollution in the atmosphere and its many potential deadly consequences, over the next 30 years up to 2021, emissions just continued to rise and we released more CO_2 into the atmosphere than the rest of our history combined: some 948 billion metric tons in just 30 years.

NOAA (The National Oceanic and Atmospheric Administration of the US) has been researching greenhouse gas levels up to 2022 and their historically high rates of growth.

Atmospheric CO2 is now 50% higher than pre-industrial levels, going from slight fluctuations around an average of around 200 ppm (parts per million) for thousands of years, to a huge rise of up to over 417 ppm in just the last few hundred years. Atmospheric methane, less abundant than CO2 but far more potent at trapping heat, having record growth in pollution levels over 2020-2021, has now increased by two and a half times its pre-industrial level. While nitrous oxide, again less abundant but over two hundred and fifty times more powerful at retaining heat than CO2, has increased by nearly 25% of it pre-industrial level, with the two highest increases being in 2020 and 2021.

About a quarter to one half of CO2 human emissions to date have been absorbed by the world's oceans, which is contributing to ocean acidification and threatening some fish populations and other aquaculture. This has caused around a 30% increase in acidity, and if these trends continue, because we continue with our rates of pollution, then the damage to marine organisms could seriously threaten the stability of many marine food chains. Recent global warming changes in climate has also caused another issue that is increasing CO2 levels in the atmosphere, as rising temperatures rapidly thaws lands in the more northern latitudes, so permafrost, that was previously frozen soil, is thawing out and releasing further greenhouse gases into the atmosphere. Although these amounts are not huge compared to our current direct human pollutions, they are significant enough to add to the increasing imbalance.

Sea ice and glaciers are now visibly melting at alarming rates around the world, due to global temperature rises brought on by pollution. The Antarctic and Greenland ice sheets contain approximately 99% of the freshwater ice on Earth; as they melt then sea levels rise, and if they both completely melted, the seas would rise by an estimated 67m. While a complete meltdown is certainly not being predicted, it does show the potential effects of ice melting in these regions; currently Antarctica is losing ice mass at 150 billion tons per year, while Greenland is losing about 270 billion tons per year (NASA statistics).

These are very significant amounts of melting ice that are contributing one-third of the total sea level rises, along with other glaciers melting and also the expansions of seas due to temperature rises caused by global warming. National Geographic reported that since 1880 average sea levels have risen around 23cm, with a rise of about 9cm in just the last 25 years, so rising levels are accelerating and these levels are very significant, considering the oceans cover 70% of the Earth's surface. These changes further effect extreme weather incidents and flooding, coastal populations and their habitats, habits of fish and where they spawn, the survival of wildlife that exists in the ice sheet regions, and the increased flooding of coastal areas around the world.

Air pollution from industrial processes, toxic waste incineration, and other burning practices is a more immediate and direct threat to human health though, already having a devastating affect on human populations. The World Health Organisation, established on 'World Health Day' in 1948 as a specialised agency of the UN to promote, monitor and improve health worldwide, has been monitoring and reporting on air quality since the 1950's. Their database, the largest of its kind, covers data from over 6000 cities and human settlements in 117 countries, and it is updated regularly every 2-3 years (since 2011). Using a Sustainable Development Goal Indicator, they hope to help to bring down levels of air pollution in time, which will need significant changes in industrial practices and world economics. This is a summary of their current overview of the world's air quality situation:

Air pollution is the largest single environmental risk to health today, estimated to be responsible for around 7 million premature deaths globally every year. Air pollution, both indoors and outdoors, is contamination of the air we breath by any chemical, physical or biological agent that modifies the natural characteristics of the atmosphere. The most harmful of these are: particulate matter (small solid or liquid particles - such as soot, dust, smokes, fumes and mists), ground level ozone (affecting human, animal and plant respiration at higher concentrations), nitrogen oxides (produced mostly by burning processes and fuel combustion) and sulfur oxides (from burning fossil fuels and processing mineral ores that contain sulfur). Increased exposure to these pollutants is linked to cardiovascular diseases (heart disease and stroke), chronic obstructive pulmonary disease, acute lower respiratory infections and lung cancer, as well as other health affects. Together these are the main causes of premature deaths in humans, due to exposure to the air pollution that we are creating.

Some cities around the world are blighted by atmospheric conditions that allow air pollutants to regularly build within the atmosphere, from industry, engine pollution and domestic cooking. Every day 93% of children around the world under 15 (1.8 billion) breathe polluted air that is putting their health and development at serious risk. WHO estimated in 2016 that around 600,000 children died from acute lower respiratory infections caused by polluted air from outside and household sources. Exposure to air pollution in women can also increase premature birth cases, low-birth weight children, and impact asthma and childhood cancer. Air pollution is one of the leading threats to child health, accounting for nearly 1 in 10 deaths in children under 5. Nearly all of these pollution issues are down to our irresponsible and extreme industrialised production economies and the lack of safe facilities for an ever increasing number of poor and impoverished populations…, all the repercussions of the control of greed psychology over our world and its focus on industry and profit.

Climate change

While some of these pollution issues have already been touched upon in this chapter in relation to their causes, it may help just to clarify them a little further in the part they currently play to the wider picture of human challenges now facing us all. Climate change has been talked about, studied and researched for many decades now, due to increasing evidence that industrial pollution was driving temperature rises. But because of differences in evidence and statistics, then scientists, governments and corporations have often ended up arguing about the finer details. Governments and businesses invested in the large scale use of fossil fuels and of industrialised farming have been able to use these disputes to try to deny the evidence and avoid taking responsibility, at least for a time, before the repercussions of climate change became too obvious and damaging to deny or ignore.

The basic science of climate change and temperature rises caused by human pollutions that change the composition of the atmosphere, is actually quite simple and indisputable. It is only in the predictions as to how much temperatures will be affected, how quickly and for how long, and how damaging they will be, that there is room for differences and possible disputes. Because dealing with the real causes of these issues requires such fundamental examinations and changes in the established psychologies and habits of our modern commercial societies and their entire economic systems, then governments have often made just token commitments to change. This has then given the public the false impression, due to a lack of real fundamental action, that it is not that serious; polluting industries just continue to roll on and even expand, while they know that the CO2 imbalances they are adding to could remain in the atmosphere for up to thousands of years and seriously affect the climates and stabilities of our world.

Transitions to non-polluting forms of energy production are minimal in comparison, and the attitude seems to be 'we'll just keep using the fossil fuels up while they are available and profitable to extract and burn; too many established businesses with economic power and influence on governmental decisions are simply making too much profit from fossil fuel usage to want to change things. In reality, greed and its desire for profit has most of the controls over our collective and essential resources, and the minority currently in charge nearly all live extremely rich and lavish lifestyles that they don't want to have to be called on and to change. Most of us now realise this after years of cover ups and deceit, regarding the true culprits of environmental damage and pollution, but those protecting their extreme privileged lifestyles currently possess most of our wealth and still hold the major decisions of control in our world, and until this changes, industry and extreme pollution just goes on.

The basic science of climate change due to human pollution is as follows (courtesy of the Met Office UK): the main cause of climate change is the burning of fossil fuels such as oil, gas and coal. When burnt, fossil fuels release carbon dioxide into the air, changing the balance of greenhouse gasses in the atmosphere, trapping in more heat from the sun, and causing the planet to heat up. And there it is, an extremely simple statement to understand and very hard to really dispute. For the past few thousand years up until the 1800's, the Earth had maintained fairly consistent average temperatures and temperature variations, between its different geological eco-systems and their various climate ranges. The stability of all the life that has evolved on our planet is dependant upon this, us included, of course. Since the 1800's, by the continued rise in the burning of fossil fuels, and in the ways that we have begun to farm and use the land for increasing livestock production, human activity has quickly become the leading cause of changes to our climate and its weather patterns.

Some gases in the Earth's atmosphere, known as greenhouse gases, act to trap heat and to stop it escaping back out into space. These gases act like a warm blanket around the Earth, which is known as the 'greenhouse effect'. Greenhouse gases exist naturally, such as carbon dioxide, methane and nitrous oxide, but they can be added to and their balance altered, by both natural and human sources. Other polluting gases, like CFCs (chlorofluorocarbons), are only produced by human methods and activity. When short-wave radiation from the sun reaches the Earth, most of it passes through the atmosphere and hits the surface, with the Earth absorbing most of this radiation and giving off longer wavelength infrared radiation. The greenhouse gases in our atmosphere then absorb some of this infrared radiation and emit further radiation in every direction. Some of this is sent back towards the Earth's surface causing it to to heat up; the more greenhouse gases in the atmosphere, then the more radiation there is towards the surface of the Earth, and the more heat can be trapped.

If you've ever walked into a small human-made glass greenhouse, used for growing plants by maintaining a warmer and more consistent environment, then the principles are very similar, and you can appreciate how hot the air can get in such a contained environment. A small human-made greenhouse allows the sun's heat and radiation to pass through the outer glass, which then gets absorbed by the soil and plants and converted to heat radiation energy which cannot easily escape back out through the glass insulation. The thicker and more insulating the glass then the more heat can potentially become trapped inside. Convection of the air in a greenhouse also helps with the increase and regulation of the heat as the warmed air rises and the cooler air drops down, and this convection cycle allows the air to absorb more heat each time. Now in smaller human-made greenhouses this can be regulated and controlled (doors, windows and fans can be used for example), but on the mass scale of our planetary atmosphere, if the trapped heat is increased, then everything connected to this starts to become affected by the increases; nature's established regulations and subsequent climate patterns and ecosystems all become destabilised, and the life that is dependent on these stabilities all begins to suffer.

The natural greenhouse effect is crucial to our survival and to most life on Earth: without the greenhouse gases then the Earth would be about 30 degrees colder on average than it is today. But with all the extra greenhouse gases that we have been pumping into the atmosphere since the industrial age began, the greenhouse effect is now heating up the planet much faster than any previous natural phenomena. This has been called the 'enhanced greenhouse effect' and it is the main cause of climate change in our world today. This heating up process can take a little time to become apparent to us, which previously made it easy for even political leaders to just deny that climate change was possible, and infer that nothing significant was happening. But in recent years the repercussions of this enhanced greenhouse affect have become obviously more apparent, and temperatures will continue to rise for many years to come, especially if we just ignorantly continue to add to the mass of greenhouse gases in our atmosphere.

The human activities we need to address that are the main causes of polluting greenhouse gas emissions, are as follows: the burning of all fossil fuels, coal, oil and gas, that release carbon dioxide into the atmosphere; Deforestation - as trees and plants store carbon dioxide from the atmosphere, and release carbon when they are burnt; Agriculture - planting more crops and rearing more livestock for growing populations and commercial profits, releases more methane and nitrous oxide into the atmosphere; and cement production - responsible for 2% of total human carbon dioxide emissions. All of the evidence is both simple common sense and now irrefutable; The Intergovernmental Panel on Climate Change has now stated unequivocally that human activity is the major cause of global warming... Now we just need to change the real fundamental issues that are escalating it, as the already established imbalances will be with us for centuries to come.

So what are the worst repercussions of climate change and rising temperatures? We have already explored the affects of sea level rises from melting ice sheets and glaciers, and from ocean expansions due to heating, but how else is it affecting our world. Well we are already seeing some of the deadly repercussions in our world today, and these are just the early stages: increased wild fires in hot areas, increased storms and irregular weather patterns, record high temperatures, heavier rain downpours and increased flooding, trees and plants dying from droughts, coral reef bleaching and deaths, crop failures from changing weather cycles. These are just a few resulting issues that clearly seem to be on the increase from year to year.

Other repercussions include: changes in the hydrological cycle (evaporation, condensation and precipitation) affecting fauna and flora, land geography and weather cycles; changing ocean currents, affecting marine species populations, behaviours and migration patterns; and warmer land and air in many areas of the planet, with many affects to all life and eco-systems. The major impacts to humans are numerous: risks to water supplies, loss of biodiversity in areas, localised and coastal flooding, fisheries failing, seasonal patterns shifting, habitat regions of pests expanding, food production instabilities, more conflict and climate migrations, heat stress and damage to eco-systems. While developed nations currently produce most of the greenhouse gas emissions, it is mostly developing nations that will first suffer from the most serious effects, with larger poorer populations and less resources to adapt. But now, right across the span of our nations and their wealth disparities, we are all starting to suffer the serious repercussions of these climate instabilities.

Regardless of the longer term predictions for how temperatures will rise and by how much, the reality is that climate change is already here and massively impacting our world. If we do not fully transition away from the fundamental causes of this, then we will all be suffering the increasingly destructive consequences for some time to come, especially our future generations. The facts are simple, the evidence is indisputable, and the resolutions are just common sense to anyone who looks with open eyes: just stop and transition all of the processes that are polluting the atmosphere. The one thing that is stopping this simple and intelligent action though, is greed, and its desire for expanding wealth and profit… Remove this from power, and the readily available resolutions can be freed up completely to do their work of redressing the imbalances.

Resource Depletion and Rising Populations:

Depletion of our natural resources and constantly rising populations are increasing the pressures of a major human challenge from both ends at the same time: some of our basic resources to live and survive are dwindling or becoming less available, while the demands for them from rising populations are ever increasing. It's another simple equation with a simple message. With all of the pressures that we have already mentioned previously on our societies and their populations, where environments are being damaged by pollution, climate changes and deforestation, and where resources are being over mined, over fished and over farmed..., then there is starting to be less of certain resources available to feed and support our expanded human populations. Add this issue to a constantly growing population and their demands, with increasing pollution and climate instabilities, and you have very high probabilities of many large scale humanitarian disasters ahead. The longer we allow capitalist greed to continue with the over production and pollution, then the worse these disasters will be for us all. When societies break down under these pressures, then panic, lawlessness and conflict can quickly ensue, and we are already beginning to see this in the poorer and more unstable countries of our world.

Water, perhaps the most essential element to life and to our survival as humans, is being depleted in its fresh and drinkable form. Only 2.5% of the water on our planet is fresh water, and most of this, for now at least, is in the form of ice and snow cover. As more natural waters and rivers become polluted and ground water contaminated by human activities, then less is available to safely drink, and with higher populations and increased demands, then people in drought or polluted areas will struggle to survive. The Food and Agriculture Organisation of the UN predicts that by

2025, up to 1.8 billion people will have no drinkable water. Populations without drinkable water often quickly succumb to illness and disease from contaminated water sources, while those without water completely have to migrate quickly of they will die.

Since the last ice age 10,000 years ago, we have lost one-third of our world's forests (various statistics taken from Our World in Data); that's two billion hectares of forest, an area twice the size of the United States. We have mostly cut down and cleared forest areas over the years for fire wood as fuel, to grow crops on the land and raise livestock, and as a raw material for building and production. Half of this loss occurred between 8,000 BCE and 1900, but since then, with population increases and industrial demands, we have cut down the other half of around one billion hectares. In the last few decades since the peak of deforestation in the 1980's, then the figures for the rates of tree loss have started to be offset by reforestation initiatives (mostly in large parts of Asia): the UN Forest Resources Assessment estimated the net losses to have fallen from just over 100 million hectares in the 1980's, to 78 million in the 1990's and 47 million in the 2010's. However, most deforestation comes from cutting down rich tropical rainforest, so even with net reductions in loss, in the 2010's we still cut down prime forest that would cover an area twice the size of Spain.

While reforestation projects are good and are helping to supply a more sustainable source of wood from plantation forests, they cannot offset the loss of biodiversity and wildlife habitat from the destruction of long established tropical forests. Mass deforestation, as we have mentioned, can have a big effect on global warming (currently around a 10% influence); less trees means less CO_2 absorbed from the atmosphere, and more clearing and burning of trees means more CO_2 and greenhouse gas pollution. The established forests of our world also have a big influence on rainfall patterns, water and soil quality, and flood prevention and soil erosion. Millions of people still rely directly on forests as their home and to make a living, and many of these are being affected and displaced by deforestation. Population increases and urbanisation in some areas of the world is also constantly adding to the pressures causing deforestation, as more people clear land for agriculture and need wood for building and fuel. Up to 15 billion trees are still being cut down every year, which is extremely damaging to people, wildlife and the environment, and is certainly not sustainable. Stopping deforestation is another huge challenge currently facing humanity, as a finite resource will always run out eventually, if we just keep using it up.

The fishing industries of our world currently catch and produce around 200 million tonnes of fish and seafood every year, which come from a combination of wild fish catch and fish farming. With the rapid development and growth of aquaculture in the last few decades, then we actually now produce more seafood from fish farms than we do from wild catch. The World Wildlife Fund reported that the natural stocks of fish that were being over fished around the world has tripled in the last 50 years, with about one third of the world's assessed fisheries currently being overfished. Fishing for a living as a food supply for our rising populations is not a bad thing, but as fishing has become industrialised and more competitive over the years, then fish are being caught faster than they can replenish, meaning there is less to catch and go around and less fish to reproduce.

Seafood populations are being hit in three main ways by human activities: commercial overfishing; pollution of the rivers and oceans, by old sea nets, sewerage, chemicals and plastics; and water climate changes and ocean current abnormalities, all affecting marine life and their reproduction cycles. Bycatch is another damaging issue threatening marine life, as many types of industrial fishing vessels now net huge hauls of all types of sea life, and much of the non-legal catch or commercially unwanted sea life dies and is cast back into the Ocean. As fish stocks are overfished and reduced then dependant livelihoods collapse, and people in coastal areas dependant on seafood as their main food source, can begin to go hungry and may be forced to migrate.

Today's worldwide fishing fleet is estimated to be two and a half times the capacity needed to catch what we actually need to eat, and this overfishing is now supported by subsidies in some countries to support industry above marine life, even though the costs of fishing may be destructive and not economically viable. Illegal fishing is another huge problem causing some of the worst impacts on the environment, as money and profit is often the only consideration of those responsible. It was estimated that unreported and unregulated fishing can net criminals up to $36 billion every year, and they have set up large hidden supply chains to protect them from detection. In all of these issues, greed is a big influence and having a great detrimental impact, damaging the sustainability of seafood resources for the wider populations now and for the world's long term future.

Finally, most of us have been made aware of the huge depletion in accessible sources of our major fossil fuels. Estimates of reserves are as follows (according to current known practical availability and usage rates): coal, about 135 years remaining, oil about 55 years and natural gas about 45 years. Maybe not a bad thing you might think, as this might force us to look elsewhere for fuel sources and really begin to invest fully in the renewable and sustainable sources that hold our only viable long term future. But this has certainly not yet been the case, as fossil fuel consumption has risen dramatically in just the last 50 years. While there is still so much dependence on fossil fuel across our world, and so much money and profit being made from their production and use, then things don't seem set to change that much, and the resulting pollution of their continued use builds within our atmosphere.

As developing nations have looked to expand their own industrial developments and economic powers over recent decades, and most of these have been based on fossil fuel consumptions, then more and more of their populations have their livelihoods dependant on these fuels. The longer we go on enabling the use of fossil fuels around the world, and using up these resources irresponsibly, then the more the pollution increases and the more pressure there is on human and environmental health. The longer we go on with this then the more the dependency grows, and the harder the transition away from fossil fuels will become, with less and less time to manage and implement this inevitable change in a smooth and practical way.

I know I have mentioned some of the pressures caused by our ever increasing population rise, as we have gone from 1 billion to 8 billion in just the last 200 years, but all of these issues of pollution, depletion and increased demand on resources are enlarged as our populations continue to grow and we continue to run industry on fossil fuels. The pressures on our essential resources are already close to breaking point in many regions of our world, so if, as the UN predicts, we start to near 10 billion by the decade 2050 onwards, then the pressures may become unimaginably difficult. The next 10-20 years of human action is crucial as to the scale of disasters ahead of us, it is unprecedented in human history; how it all unfolds is very much within our hands and our responsibility.

Environmental Damage and Falling Wildlife Populations

As a kind of summary to this chapter, we can have a brief look at some of the realities that greed and extreme commercialism have put upon our world over their dominance of the last two centuries. With the issues of climate and weather instabilities, rising sea levels, land, water and air pollution, depleting resources and rising populations, the challenges to humans are extensive…, but the challenges to our environments and their eco-systems, and to all of the biodiversity and wildlife that inhabit these, is also a huge threat to life and future populations. There is still so much that we don't yet know about how many species of animals, insects and plants there are on Planet Earth, especially in the less explored regions of our rain forests, and a large amount of this biodiversity may actually be being wiped out before we have really had a chance to study and appreciate it.

The World Wildlife Fund reported in recent years that the rapid loss of species in our recent modern era, due mainly to increased human actions upon the environment, is estimated to be between 1000 and 10,000 times higher than the normal extinction rates of natural evolution. This equates to between 0.01 and 0.1% of all species being forced into extinction each year. This doesn't sound like much at first, but put into context, if the lower estimate of there being 2 million species on our planet is accurate, then that means we could be causing 200 - 2,000 extinctions every year. But if the higher estimates are more accurate, of there potentially being up to 100 million species on our planet, then that means potentially 10,000 to 100,000 species falling into extinction every year. Either way, although these are just potential estimates, the numbers are extreme and disturbing, and the more species become extinct, then the more affect this can have on the established eco-systems, with knock-on affects to many other species.

According to the IUCN (International Union for the Conservation of Nature) more than 41,000 species in our world are currently under threat of extinction; with global wildlife populations falling as much as 69% on average since 1970. The main threats that our actions have imposed upon species are these: the destructive influences of pollution and global warming; habitat destruction, loss and degradation; unsustainable hunting methods; the human introduction of non-native species to different eco-systems; and the spreading of diseases that kill native wildlife. Of course, not everyone understands the importance of maintaining good and natural biodiversity; nature has been evolving and establishing its eco-systems for far longer than humans have been around and could imagine. Where human existential activities and demands take priority for livelihoods and survival, then there can often be conflict with local species and biodiversity, and sometimes with conservation initiatives.

So it's not just the larger more talked about species that are under threat, like the rhinos, leopards, tigers, gorillas, orangutangs and elephants; species extensions means whole hosts of plants, animals and insects disappearing from food chains. A study by the Royal Botanic Gardens in conjunction with Kew and Stockholm University, looking at plant extinctions over the last 250 years, found that 571 species of plants had completely disappeared from the wild, and that due to human activities, plant extinctions are occurring up to 500 times faster than average natural rates. The destruction of native plant habitats on a large scale can also have a devastating effect on insect populations and pollination cycles. As well as habitat loss, both pesticides and air pollution are affecting many of the insects and other pollinating animals, and with less pollination there are less plants. Bee populations have been notably in decline over recent years: globally we have lost one-quarter of our 20,000 bee species since 1990 (Independent), and of around 100 crop species in UK farming, bees pollinate around 70 of these (Revive a Bee). So you can imagine the consequences of important bee species dying out, and due to humans, numbers are in decline globally.

Wow, so many statistics, and so much to take in in just one chapter, listed together it can all seem very dire and frightening; perhaps too frighting for some to really look at and to try to fully take in, so it's hard to know how to react. It may seem like all doom when it is listed together in one chapter or piece of literate, but I would like to add a quick reminder of the counterbalance, that there is still so much that is positive in humanity and in our developing consciousness and communities. If we can identify on a global scale and take out the destructive elements (fear, greed, extreme capitalist thinking), to agree to found everything we do on sustainability, then we do have a potentially prosperous future ahead of us. But it will require a monumental collective effort of change, now and in the coming decades; a genuine step forward in our evolution as a species. It requires a real committed change in the priorities of our core and base animal instincts: from selfish thinking of just individual survival, to the collective thinking of the wellbeing and continuation of all humanity and life in balance; only then, can we begin to call ourselves intelligent.

There are probably good sounding counter arguments for much of what I have presented here; capitalism and greed have needed and developed these over the years, to try to survive and to keep the majority of us turning the wheels of production, and in the age of information and disinformation these tactics have often worked. People choose to believe what suits them best or what they are force fed over the years of media and education control. Nothing can change the real facts, however, and these issues listed here, regardless of the little percentage differences in statistics and estimates, are all genuine global scale problems now facing humanity and causing damage and destruction.

Virtually all of these issues are growing and they will certainly all have to be faced and addressed at some point, it is just a question of when, and how bad we let things get before we really act collectively. There will a global breaking point at some stage in the future; it is impossible to known what the balance will be between the increasing extremes of pollution and destruction, and the realisation of our need to fundamentally change: how bad will the climate and environmental suffering need to become, before we collectively react?

As we continue to allow the controls of our world to remain in the hands of the diseased and greedy minds of a minority of elite rich and wealthy leaders of business and government, then we are enabling the destruction and pollution to go on; most of these people only really care about their own images and their own more immediate gratifications, there is no real thought for the long term future of the planet and its general wider populations. Collectively the generations of the last 2 centuries can hold their hand up and say 'we did that', 'we allowed that to happen on our watch', 'we let greed take a hold on humanity'. Will we allow the generations of now and the future to be able to say, 'we were the ones who really turned things around'?

These are of course just general outlines on pollution and the many issues that humanity now faces, they are just simplified figures on paper that can be discarded and forgotten easily, if they are not related to the real experience of the world outside and the possible futures we are all facing. I appreciate this is far from a comprehensive study; if you want to research further then there are numerous sources, studies and reports available, they have been being written and presented as warnings for decades now. Governments and business leaders may argue and disagree about the precise statistics, which has only served to distract from and delay the real committed long term action that is needed. To argue about statistics is just to miss the real point: these are all genuine and real issues of our own making, already creating long term damage, and they will all, without question, have to be faced up to.

So now we will go on to really look at and explore the positive options ahead of us as a race; to see how we can genuinely change the fundamentals of our societies from the fear and greed that has created so many disastrous issues, and to really begin to turn the tide towards a more balanced planet, and a better and fairer humanity for all.

Chapter 11: Exploring The Solutions to Healing the Disease

Where do you begin when looking at a diseased psychology that has grown from something so primal and innate in all human beings, that has branched out and grown into the minds and behaviours of humans over thousands of years, and has come to build and establish strongholds in all of our positions of power and control over resources and government? What genuinely can be done to heal and turn such a disease around? If you look back through history, it has always been there, if you look at our world today, then its influence is everywhere; so how do you go about removing something this deep set and established? There are certainly no quick fixes and no easy solutions that will instantly transform every problem and issue. Long term behavioural issues will need fundamental changes in our psychologies and long term recovery and supports, and these often begin and are brought into action through dramatic, sometimes catastrophic and revelational experiences and realisations: where we are left with no choice but to change things.

Well we have started and have been working on solutions for several decades now, to the many issues that capitalist greed has created; mainly because we have started to realise and are having to deal with the very real repercussions of these issues in our world. To begin with, the investigative journalism and environmentalist movements that have grown and developed since the 1960's have played a big part in revealing the corrupt and destructive elements of greed in our governments and large corporations. This has helped to make people more aware of what has really been going on in our world and to some of the more sinister reasons behind certain wars, economic decisions and corporate profiteering.

These early voices and movements for greater transparency and equality, and for more environmental responsibility, then went on to inspire more generations. In the early 1970's the first 'Earth Day' was celebrated, leading to the creation of the United States Environmental Protection Agency, The National Environmental Policy Act was passed by Congress, the National Resources Defence Council was established, the National Oceanographic and Atmospheric Administration was set up, DDT (a toxic chemical widely used in pesticides) was banned, the Clean Water Act, Marine Mammal Protection Act and Coastal Zone Management Act were all implemented, and Greenpeace was founded in 1971, an environmental group dedicated to challenging and exposing environmental damage and pollution by human activity and ignorant governments and corporations.

The lists of environmental protection acts, movements and campaigns has increased ever since across the globe, and alongside these and many on-going research projects that monitor our environments, then investments have started to flow into all of the alternative and non-polluting types of energy production, and into more sustainable and environmentally friendly ways to build, produce food and live. Technologies of wind, solar and hydroelectric power have all developed and improved, huge advances have been made in heat source pumps and building insulations, electric vehicles and transport systems, and new processes of more sustainable farming, like regenerative farming and organic farming. This has all supported a genuine rise in Green political movements; we now have many strong voices and advocates for the welfare of the environment, and for greater fairness and equality in wealth distribution to invest in all communities for the longer term.

With all of the challenging issues we are currently facing in our world, we now have all of the knowledge and technologies to really impact and turn around the environmental destruction and pollution that is taking place, and to invest in and establish large systems of green energy production and global sustainable living. We also already have millions of people calling out for these changes and willing to help to implement them. For all of this knowledge and these advances though, there is still one major problem that exists, holding back and denying our full transitions to the green sustainable living that is essential for our future stability: most of the control of our essential resources and of our world economics and governments are still in the hands of an elite rich, infected by the psychologies of greed, control and domination. For all of these destructive issues in our world on the surface, at the heart of all these issues, the real root cause is the selfish weakness of fear and greed.

Greed has mastered a control of our world's systems over many centuries, and the infected thinking of greed is passed on through each generation: the aristocracies and wealthy elites pass this on through inheritance and bloodlines, and the controls of resources and wealth are handed on through small societies of the elite rich, in ownership and corporate directorships. Greed has a stronghold on our world's systems through a tiny minority of elite wealthy advocates of these extreme disparities, and as greed is a narcissistic and potentially psychopathic disease of the mind, then admitting responsibility and handing wealth, power and control over to those who are more balanced and responsible, to more fairly manage our resources, is not an option for a greed dominated mind. You cannot stop or heal a disease by just trying to deal with its repercussions on the surface; the source of greed will still remain within its human hosts, and as history has shown, it will always adapt and find new channels. Greed has to be dealt with at its root source for our world to really change, and for the controls to be freed up and released.

As has been mentioned previously, the thinking of greed has managed to establish itself in a wider field of human thinking through the philosophies of capitalism. It has adapted to create moderately comfortable middle classes in many developed nations, who might be well educated and feel more invested in capitalism, to think this might protect their own smaller amounts of wealth and property. Our governments and economies are now so dependant upon and controlled by capitalist systems, that most countries political parties stand for the same industrial and commercial economics; their different promises are more about how they propose to share out the wealth than about how sustainably it is produced. So voting options are often restricted, or even manipulated in poorer developing countries, and people are caught up in the voting habits of the limited choices of well established traditional parties.

What we still lack is a collective majority of people freed up to see the real nature of greed and what it is currently doing to our world, who then have a viable green and sustainable voting option to bring power and wealth controls out of the hands of the elite rich. So many of the general populations of our world's nations are simply too caught up in the living and survival demands of life to have the time to look for, believe in and vote for real sustainable and fairer alternatives. They are just living life and trying to make the best of things, working long hours and paying their bills. Many people have become disillusioned with politics and politicians, making their promises for votes during their pre-election campaigns, but then rarely changing anything fundamentally, because the greed controlling our global economic systems simply won't allow for real fundamental changes.

Capitalism is big business and it has the best paid lawyers, political promoters and advertising and social media at its disposal. It has often tried to paint positive sustainability parties and green energy activism as extremist and anti-capitalist, as is if being anti-capitalist in your philosophies is somehow an evil and unpatriotic. For most people looking towards greener alternatives in politics, anti-capitalism is actually about pro-sustainability and the fair distribution of wealth amongst all populations; it does not mean anti-business or anti-ingenuity or anti-technology, it just means that all these things are done sustainably and in balance with the environment and our resources, and that nobody profits unfairly or disproportionately from these things. Anti-capitalist just means anti-greed, anti-destruction and pollution and anti-control of mass global resources by small rich elites. Anti-capitalist means pro-humanity, pro-healthy environments and pro-common sense and intelligence.

Sadly, at present, most of the transitions and controls to new sustainable technologies and green energy production are being directed by large private companies and corporations; some of these also being connected with fossil fuel production and profits, where they look to sound greener but actually act in support of continuing more with fossil fuel use. While it is great that cleaner, greener energy is being invested in and expanding its ability to produce and supply clean energy, if the controls are not publicly governed, then profits can be removed for personal gains instead of being fully reinvested, and dependencies can still be created that means populations can be held to ransom. Privately owned companies that prioritise profit usually try to control and monopolise markets as much as they can, as this allows them to control and build more profits, and the thinking of greed can very easily become dominant.

Although a simple analogy based around a game, many of today's generations will be familiar with the board game Monopoly, which is a perfect simplified example of capitalist thinking and greed psychology, brought into the experience of over 1 billion people. Over 250 million games have been sold in 47 different languages, across 114 countries (Business Insider), and it is the number one board game in the US and one of the most popular in history. But if we just think about the aims of the game for a moment, then the psychologies are very revealing as to its extreme capitalist principles. The main aim of the game is to buy up and control properties, rail networks and water and electricity companies, and then to demand increasing rents from people who land on your properties. Gradually you look to buy out other players' properties and force them into bankruptcy through increasing developments and rent costs, so that eventually there is only one winner… with all of the properties, all of the money and all of the controls. The game can often lead to upset and arguments amongst its players with the ruthless tactics required to win, and although it is just a game for entertainment, it is a good reflection of the exact thinking of extreme capitalism.

The nature of greed as a disease of the mind is that once people have such a psychological illness, that is narcissistic and often psychopathic, they don't actually recognise their illness or self-analyse. They may seem convincing, even charming, in speaking, especially if involved in leadership or politics, but they can lack any ability to truly empathise with other people and their situations. People fully infected with the imbalance of greed always believe they are right, infallible, and are driven by their deeper fear compulsions to keep seeking money and power. Their behaviours are out of their control in this respect, and they will believe they are justified in their thoughts of convincing others of their right to privilege and of their superiority.

The psychology and impulses of greed, once they have taken hold of the thoughts of an individual, can rarely be controlled; it is an unconscious mental illness that works behind the direct self-awareness of a person, which enables them to undertake unconscionable actions without the slightest hint of conscience or remorse. Examples of this are: destroying the livelihoods of others, allowing the pollution of lands that people depend on for survival, authorising and instigating wars and the slaughter of other peoples, and amassing unreasonably large amounts of wealth and assets by profiteering off of the labour of others; all actions that the disease of greed has led to.

This is the reality of greed we are up against, in that it has a hold of and directs the minds of most of those who currently control the vast majority of our world's resources: those who run private banks and have economic influence, those on the boards of large corporations with market dominance, and those who champion capitalist politics and direct governments. To fully remove this type of greed from its hold over humanity, then we have to trace and deal with it at the very root of its origin. Any disease of the mind is like a weed: it starts with a seed, a trauma or root source of thought (usually fear based), that if left unattended and unresolved, can then grow and spread out within the mind to have more and more influence on thinking and perception, and to gradually take more control of the mind and its impulses of action. If we just try to deal with all of the repercussions of the actions of greed within our world, then for one, we will have our hands extremely full and occupied, but essentially, the root and source of the greed will remain and keep growing through again, as it always has throughout our history.

At the root of greed and all the actions of control and dominance that it can lead to, there is just weakness and fear. It is a weakness of the mind in human nature that can then let in fear to fully take over the thinking and actions of a person, if they choose to allow it to. The fears that relate to our innate instincts of survival can then become exaggerated on an ever expanding scale: our fears of scarcity, suffering, being dominated, having pain inflicted, being killed, all leading to the ultimate fear of the ego, which is death and its own mortality. And fear demands a reaction, or some form of compensation to be appeased. Those infected by greed psychologies can genuinely think they are justified in their imbalanced actions and profiteering; you may see them as sounding articulate and they have created a political environment in our current modern world where their extremes present themselves as normal and acceptable.

In the exaggeration of all of these fears within the mind to the extreme, then all thinking and behaviours look to compensate to the extreme, to try to protect the weakness of the person and ego which is programmed to react and survive. All of these fears then become turned around in reactionary thinking and behaviours that seek to compensate: the fear of scarcity in turned into the impulses of seeking control of wealth and resources, and to building and hoarding as much as possible, as in fear, enough can never be enough; the fear of being dominated and subjugated leads to the impulses to dominate and subjugate others; while the fear of suffering and pain can project outwards as actions that can inflict suffering and pain on others, seemingly without remorse, as the reactionary thoughts believe they are dealing with a justified threat; the fear of being killed and having everything taken then compensates by initiating the killing of others first and taking what they have, expanding out to war, colonisations and genocides.

When fear is allowed to take hold of the mind in this way then the person becomes convinced that it is real, and they can feel driven and fully justified in their compensation behaviours to protect themselves, no matter how inhumane and extreme their behaviours might become. Fear imagines that this is what others would do to them, so it reacts first, and when fear takes over thinking, then it becomes all about the self and self-survival, so all empathy and feeling for others, who have now become perceived as a threat, is lost. These fears and their many reactionary behaviours taken to their extremes, that we have examined and explored throughout this book, is what I have described as the disease of greed. This is the real root of most of our world's imbalances that needs to be identified and removed, and this book is aimed at helping to understand and identify greed, for only we, collectively, can choose to remove it from power.

The list of reactionary behaviours then goes on; it is very easy to see the root cause when you can understand how it all works through opposite reactionary behaviours: the fear of being made to feel inferior, leads to a desire to make yourself feel superior; the fear of feeling insignificant or unnoticed, leads to the desire to become famous or perhaps infamous; the fear of not having enough, leads to the desire to have more and more; the fear of death, leads to the desire to find some miracle longevity and to imprint actions upon the world that might mean immortality in historic memory. The irony of allowing fear to take a hold of your mind and thinking is that rather than free you from these fears and all of the horrors that they can conjure as possible threats, actually listening to and taking fear in to your mind to control your reactions, then puts you in a world controlled and shaped by fear.

This can mean that you actually become stuck in the psychology of fear and cut off from feeling the true reality of the world outside, which can lead to psychosis, narcissism and psychotic behaviours. To allow fear to take over thinking is to give your time and creative energy to fear, to often enable the realisations of those fears, and this you will see everywhere in the current realities of the world around us. The fears that have taken a hold of so much of our world through the controlling minds of greed, have actually created the living realities of those fears, in the host of imbalances and threats that we are all now experiencing and having to face. Being dominated by and following the thinking and behaviours of extreme fear, means that your perceptions and judgements all become based on fear. The fear that is actually the programming to help us survive, in its many extremes and their corresponding compensations, has actually become the programming that is killing and destroying us.

When you can see it in this simplicity, stripped of all the complex growths and channels of its repercussions, then you have found and exposed the very heart and root of the problem and disease; the only place that it can truly be challenged and the tide can be turned. The solution to the damage, pollution and disparity that greed is causing in our world is actually about overcoming the fear that is behind it and our fear of actually standing up to these extreme behaviours of greed. 'Feel the fear but do it anyway', in this respect, actually means to accept that the fear responses are there within us, trying to push us to react, but rather than be controlled by these programmed selfish responses, we can actually overcome them and act for the collective good… to begin to evolve beyond them. This has already begun to happen in our species, in that we can choose to put the wellbeing of the collective and of the life on this planet, before our own self-interests and fears. This is where genuine intelligence lies, for the prosperity of the life and environments around us that support us, means the prosperity of ourselves and of all future generations.

This book and all of its chapters has primarily been about fully exposing the extreme greed psychology and imbalance in our behaviours, and tracing this back to its root and source. If you can take the time to expose and remove the root, then everything that has grown from this will begin to die out. Without the root source the disease will not be able to spread and propagate again. Healing greed is not just about the individuals who have been taken over by it, and who are directly and indirectly damaging our planet and abusing the rights of the majority of the general populations; if you remove one of these from power or their position of control, then there will quickly be somebody else to replace them. Those infected with the mental illness of greed are just weak and fearing animals, following the programming of fear that they have allowed to take ahold of their minds. As humans, those infected with fear have as much right to help and a fair living as anyone else, but they do not have a right to damage and destroy the environments of this world, or to hoard huge amounts of resources and wealth for themselves, while others go without and die as a result.

Until we realise this more collectively, and really start to work together as a majority to remove the controls and extreme privileges from those who have been abusing them due to greed imbalances, then real fundamental change will not be able to take place and establish itself in our social frameworks and forms of government. This has never been about creating an us and them divide between the extreme elite rich and the majority of the poor in our world, those divides have already been made and exist as a blatant reality when you really look. This is actually about changing the neurological programming of fear in the human race, to get us to overcome our historic enmities, our paranoias about what others may take from us, and our selfish fears to just survive at any cost.

    Real fundamental change is about being able to move past this fear control: to understand that our best prosperity and survival lies in us all working together as one race; to build sustainable and fair and equal systems that reinvest everything in improving society; and to create systems of living that work with our environments and enable them to flourish. Simple common sense tells us that we would all benefit from this, and we have all of the knowledge for this to be implemented, we just do not yet have the collective unity to make it a realty. This is where the turning of the tide needs to begin.

    I am aware this all may sound very idealistic, and some may feel they have heard these ideologies before in similar forms, but this is not a political proposal of revolution or enforced change, this is about a genuine change in human nature and its need to evolve, something that I believe circumstance will eventually necessitate. Sustainability and clean environmental living is not really about a different option or political agenda that we can choose to take or leave; we are learning from very real and hard experience that sustainability and a balanced environment holds the only realistic long term future for us all. It really is the most simple and obvious common sense and logic that even our younger children can understand from the earliest ages of learning: if you damage and use up the resources you need to live, then you will struggle and suffer.

    Decades of investigative journalism and a rise of green political movements and environmental groups have certainly helped to fully expose the realities of what greed is doing to our planet; if you want to know, it is now out there for all to see. So what we are left with now, is how to unite more people in the understanding of how we can turn this pollution, exploitation and destruction around. It is a huge global undertaking of mammoth proportions, and it is very easy to feel you might give up before you even start, especially if you are trapped in cycles of physical and financial survival that take up all your time and energy. But stopping greed and turning its damaging issues around, is not something that will ever just go away or leave us alone; issues are only getting worse because they are not being addressed and we will all be increasingly damaged and affected by inaction. We need to get to a point where any pollution of the air and land, and any profiteering and disproportionate gains of wealth are considered a crime.

So how can such a challenge really be faced up to and turned around to actually change our human nature and its responses to fear, and to take humanity a step forward in their thinking and evolution; can this really happen and be brought about? Now that we really know greed and the root of its source, then it is up to us to remove its influence on the controls of our resources and economies, there is really no other way to turn the tide. Small transitions may help upon the surface, but they will not change the fundamental foundations, and it is these that really need to change and progress.

The two main actions that we will need to follow through on then, to free us from the hold that greed currently has over humanity, are to unite and to change how resources are managed and shared. We need to find a way to globally unite in overcoming our fear, that will allow us to fully recognise and confront greed and all of the imbalances it has created in our world, and then to take all of the power and controls of our world's resources and economies out of the hands of individuals who can abuse such power and profiteer from it. We will then be able to ensure, by new laws and democratic legislation, that all essential life resources and world economies are publicly owned, fairly shared and run sustainably.

There are three main elements that can affect how this transpires in the years ahead of us. Firstly, we continue as we are for an unknown amount of time, where the pollution, destruction and exploitation continues and gets progressively worse, and those who hold the controls refuse to relinquish power and hand over their hold, so there is more potential for social collapse and conflict. Secondly, we experience more and more of the increasing effects of pollutions and climate change: rising sea levels, extremes and changes of weather patterns causing more floods and affecting food production, rising temperatures causing more forest fires and droughts, and increasing health issues with air, land and water pollution; all of these experiences increasing the pressures for us to take notice and really implement the fundamental changes that are needed. And finally, we continue to unite more behind conscientious leadership and green environmental movements, to vote-in alternatives to capitalism and greed and fully turn our economies around, to be founded on sustainability, clean energy and clean and practical production.

Unfortunately, due to the first of these elements (the continuing as we are for now, with just minor transitions to sustainability), then things are set to get much worse before they can begin to get better. A big part of our learning, and the force that will help us to all become involved in turning the tide on extreme capitalism and greed, will undoubtedly be us suffering the consequences of our actions more, due to the extreme pollution we have created, the environmental degradation and damage, and the increasing climate instabilities. With our continued inaction, sadly, all of these issues are getting worse, and will continue to create more and more instabilities and suffering, and to take more and more lives. How bad it will get before enough of us collectively can instigate a turn around in the fundamentals of our global systems of government and economics, there is no way of knowing, but this immediate element of our future does not look good.

For those who are most vulnerable, who are stuck in poverty and struggling to survive, the slightest changes in their climates, environments and economics, could be the difference between life and death; any positive changes and improvements would be immediately supported and welcomed. But for many in more developed nations who may be caught up in the daily distractions, challenges and comforts of a more privileged lifestyle, the instinct to try to stay secure in this, and to 'protect your lot', may at first hold back the realisation of the unavoidable need for fundamental change in our unsustainable and destructive economic systems. Unfortunately, most people, if they are getting by in their world, will not wholeheartedly commit to real change until trouble is actually knocking on their door and threatening their lives in some way. With the issues that have been mentioned, of pollution, dwindling resources and climate change, then trouble is coming to knock on all of our doors in the years ahead (if it hasn't begun to already), it is just a case of how bad it has to get, before enough of us feel forced to take action.

These people in the middle, that could mostly be grouped within the working class and middle class populations, are possibly the key to real democratic and lasting changes in governments and legislation, to outlaw the destructive actions and controls of greed, and to vote in a world of genuine fairness and sustainability. These middle classes will be more likely to invest in voting during elections and may have more opportunities to do so, while poorer nations with struggling populations may fall into mass migrations, chaos and revolutions more, as situations become more immediately desperate for their literal survival.

There are several difficulties when trying to vote in new greener principles of government, however, as this can be slow and take place over generational changes in perspective: many of the working and middle classes in developed nations are often stuck in traditional voting habits, caught between just two or three major established parties, so it takes time for new ideas and parties to become established and viable. It is not an easy thing for people to realise that their previous limited political options were all controlled by capitalist economies and their greed psychologies, which is what fundamentally needs to be changed for a fairer sustainable future.

This all adds to the unknowns of our immediate future across the globe; people in working and middle classes have long been kept hidden from the truths of what capitalist government economics has been enabling, regarding pollution levels and environmental destruction. Most people are kept distracted and occupied by the day to day demands of life, and people's voting decisions may be tied to their own small personal wealth gains or to the charisma and presented image of party leaders, as opposed to the the deeper political strategies of a party and what these are enabling behind the scenes. When you vote for a political party, you are voting to enable their social and economic policies, across their entire practices (what they advertise to win your votes, but also what they hide, to increase their own wealth), you are never just voting for a personality or leader. These faces will always change, and sometimes, in parties with internal conflicts of ambition, in quick succession.

Until our voting habits and priorities can change on a large scale, then greener politics based on equality and sustainability will struggle to gain power. Green politics is very much on the rise, as more people experience and realise just how unstable our climates, environments and economics are around the world, and finally understand that change is inevitable and desperately needed sooner rather than later. With the unknowns of these three main elements of how our world is moving forwards in the now (continuing as before, increasing social and climate instabilities, and the gradual shift and support for more conscientious and green movements), then it is impossible to see just how our transitions to sustainable and clean living will be enabled or forced: will we be able to do this more willingly by unity and collaboration, or will increasing climate disasters and suffering eventually force us into changing, out of the sheer necessity for survival? It's hard to know what the balance will be, and only time will tell. How this all unfolds is down to us, and how much intelligence we show collectively as a race.

It may well be, that if voting in green and sustainable policies into the heart of our governments and economies is too slow, to begin effectively counteracting the increasing sufferings of pollution and climate instabilities, that at some point there will need to be emergency world summits. As conditions under our current governments' global environmental agreements continue, those of 'make the right promises, but continue as before regarding fossil fuel pollutions and unsustainable capitalism', then situations and climate and population disasters may become so dire, as to leave no other options. We will have to come together and to work together to take full responsibility at some point, to genuinely learn our lessons regarding where greed and games of profit take us to… and to eventually realise what is most essential in sustaining a prosperous life and planet, which enables our existence and survival.

All of these three main elements though, that are forcing and instigating the changes we need, are already acting together to increase our awareness and to help us to realise that we all need to act in whatever positive way we can; no matter how small, positive action points our minds in a forward direction, and collectively it will make a difference. We also have many strong voices and environmental pioneers, who are fully committed to keep speaking out and to supporting positive changes towards fairness, sustainability and environmental protection. My thanks goes out to the likes of Rachel Carson, Wallace Broecker, David Suzuki, Bill Mckibben, Paul Hawken, David Attenborough, and Greta Thunburg (to name just a very few), for initially bringing more awareness to us regarding our environments, and for encouraging us to face the real issues that are before us. Anyone who has stood up for the environment and for greater fairness and equality, has been a hero for humanity, and has contributed to the truth getting out to the wider population. But this is just the first step, revealing and getting the truth out there, the rest is up to us, the collective population; without our unity and support, then democratically, nothing will fundamentally change, and we are all equally important in this as we move forwards.

As I have said previously, there have been numerous lives dedicated to researching and revealing the truth about pollution and environmental destruction, and there have been hundreds of books and detailed scientific papers written on these issues. This book, while briefly outlining these issues, is more about what I believe is the real legitimate source and reason behind all of these issues: extreme human fear that has developed into the psychological imbalances and disease of human greed. While greed is often mentioned and highlighted as a cause to human injustices and environmental issues, I am certain that its hold on and control of humanity is extensive, and that none of our movements of environmentalism and sustainability will be able to fully achieve their aims, until greed is fully addressed and removed from any control of human psychology and our systems of government. History has proved this to us over the centuries, where the dominance, fear and violence instigated by greed returns again and again, to destroy our peaceful ideologies and societies.

Greed, once it has taken hold of a mind and its reasoning, can then become completely ruthless in its pursuits of power and control, it may do anything to achieve its aims, and it has taken humanity into the depths of its greatest depravities. In lawless societies and criminal organisations, greed will kill, murder, rape, torture and enslave to get what it wants. If you try to stand up to and challenge this type of criminal greed, then it may end your life and put a bullet into your head without a second thought, and this is a powerful threat and deterrent to keep people in-line and silenced.

In our modern and law abiding sections of society, then greed has adapted to manipulate positions of power and control, and has been able to turn and use the law in its favour: protecting its dominance and ownerships of lands and resources, creating financial practices that enable legal profiteering, and having armies and police forces that can protect their unfairly created rights to disproportionate wealth and ownership. Here, greed has talked to us and made false claims and promises, whilst hiding the truth of its pollution and destruction, and until now, it has been able to get us to just go along with its agendas. Only we, as a united and more intelligent collective can change this reality.

There are no justifications for the controls and actions of greed, there is no need for anyone to own and possess any more than they need to live comfortably; in stable, sustainable societies, any excesses, that are currently being taken as personal profit, could offer much more stability if they were continually shared and reinvested in improving our communities and all of their amenities. Greed has taken the best of human ingenuity over the years and often used it against humanity: in wars, weapons of destruction and the arms industry; in explorations that enabled colonisations, slavery and genocides; and in the extreme contrasts between the insanely wealthy and the billions of poor struggling to survive and doing nearly all of the labour. None of this needs to be this way or can ever be reasonably justified, it's just how we have evolved and what we have chosen to create and allowed to be. How we choose to adapt and evolve into the future is down to us alone, this is one truth that we cannot debate or deny responsibility for.

When we come to live within extreme circumstances and disparities, then we can start to accept extreme behaviours as common and perhaps even 'normal': people popularised through the media with obscene amounts of wealth, flying themselves around in personal jets, or touring on their giant super yachts, while at the very same time, millions of others around the world struggle to survive, and die of poor health and poor air and water quality. It has been easy for the elite rich to deny any responsibility, many are just having too good a time to care, but somewhere along the line, directly or indirectly, these two extremes are connected, and not only by the disparities of how we currently allow wealth to be shared. In a finite world of resources, if some have excessively more, then others will have considerably less; it's a very simple and straightforward equation.

In the light of these extremes becoming seemingly common place and even 'normalised', so the ways to more equal and sustainable living can then seem a great distance away, and the changes needed to transfer to these more balanced ways could themselves be described as extreme. While fundamental shifts to non-polluting sustainable ways of living could seem ambitious and a long way off, this is only because our current systems of government and economics are so extremely unbalanced and unsustainable. There is no one solution to resolve every issue that the extremes of greed have created within the current human experience, but removing the psychologies of greed from all of our systems of control and government is essential for making genuine transitions to balanced sustainable living.

We have the knowledge and technology to make the transitions we need, we have the people power, initiative and labour, and we have the ideas and willingness to respond to the challenges facing us. All we have left to do is to break the long established thinking and habits of greed, that have built up the dependencies on and controls of our modern commercial societies. We can then prioritise thinking in terms of genuine equality for all peoples, and the global benefit and environmental prosperity of all of our actions and systems of government. We can base everything we do on non-pollution and sustainability, as we remove all capabilities for extreme profiteering and excessive personal wealth; for when there is no more reason or purpose to generate ever increasing profit margins, then thinking returns to focus upon producing what is practical and sustainable for the long term. Then our societies and communities might really begin to grow and flourish, as they have always had the potential to do and we have always professed to aim for in our political promises.

When we set the foundations of thinking within all the infrastructures of our societies, as to create the best and most efficient that we can imagine and achieve, and to continually reinvest and improve this year upon year, then it's not hard to imagine just how good life could become. Instead of the motivations of competition where one business looks to expand and dominate others, smaller businesses can coexist, support each other and share markets in a sustainable way. With no ability to 'steal' money via the control of markets and prices, to enable the currently legal profiteering of today's extreme capitalism (purely for excessive personal gains and wealth), then our motivations and incentives can become more balanced and community based: better social systems and environments that everyone can enjoy and benefit from, with the real experiences of improvement and wellbeing being able to generate its own momentum.

If we are conscientious to ensure these new social systems are managed by those who inspire and champion equality, and continually invest in and encourage a diversity of improvements and imagination through education and human creativity, then who knows the limits of what we can discover and achieve; it opens the possibility to a whole new chapter in our human evolution. At our best, when our energy is freed up of subjugation and suffering, then we are passionate, ingenious and inventive. We only need to put an end to greed and to put our power and resources in the right hands to truly begin to flourish: environmental champions, sustainability advocates, pioneers of global equality, humanitarian leaders… people with no interest in personal profits and extreme wealth… people free of the disease of human greed.

This is what can help to inspire the changes we need in our psychologies of living across the entire globe. This is what can help to heal the scars of greed and finally enable us to move beyond the programming of fear, to become one unified race. The time of distractions, dithering and ignoring is coming to an end: the time for real action is here.

There is one further element that could support our transition away from the selfish and destructive psychologies of greed and all of the extreme challenges that we are now having to face, and that is the possibility that we are not actually alone; we are not just an accident of colliding particles that just happened to start to stick together; that maybe, just maybe, there is a form of creative intelligence and purpose behind our direction and explorations of evolution and consciousness?

This is something that perhaps we will have to discover for ourselves as we continue to think and evolve, something that we may genuinely have more time for when we are no longer caught up in the conflicts of fear and of fighting and taking from each other, something that may become more collectively revealed as we step forward, as a new, more intelligent human being…

Chapter 12 : A More Intelligent Human Being

This final chapter has been added to hopefully help redress the balance between positive and negative perspectives. So much of this book has had to deal with the very difficult and sometimes disturbing aspects of greed, in the exploitation of nature and of other humans, the violence of wars, the inhumane criminal excesses of the black markets, and the long list of extreme challenges that we all now are facing in the pollution and instabilities of our world. It's a lot to take in over the course of just one book, and yet it only just scratches the surface as regards the harsher details of it all.

Millions of people are struggling in poverty for survival right now as you read these very words, and every moment of every day that passes. Some might say that this is just part of the cycle of life: birth, struggle for survival, and death. But we do all have choices and options afforded to us by the evolution of our consciousness and conscience, so we can create, plan and organise things, to make the cycle as pleasant or as horrific as we choose. We can make the cycle a more shared experience of support and equality, or a selfish and divided experience of inequality and conflict.

There are definitely questions that are raised here in our ability to individually and collectively choose our future direction; what is behind our creation and existence and how has this come to be formed and guided? Is there a creative intelligence behind the Universe, and more specifically, behind the evolution and direction of humans? No person has the right to force their own personal beliefs onto another as these are questions for individual contemplation, but it is important, when considering the continued evolution of human beings and where developments may be made, to consider all of the options and possibilities behind our direction and our impulses to evolve. This chapter looks to explore what might be considered as some of the more positive possibilities of our continued evolution; aspects that we may already have within us in their early stages of development, and ones that may become more central to our societies and their psychologies as we step beyond the primitive dominance of fear and greed, and begin to become a more intelligent human being.

It will certainly be no easy task to move away from the dominant animal instincts of some many millions of years, but the transitions in human nature and thinking have already been taking place over several thousands of years of our most recent history. The growth and development of philosophies and ethics, the religious searches for some kind of creator that we can relate to and maybe communicate with, the scientific discoveries of structure, laws and directives to the physical world of creation, and the simple human sensitivity of empathy and love. While separate books have been written about all of these subjects many thousands of times over, they all point towards a greater sense of us as a collective race, a greater connection and sensitivity between our minds, starting to feel for each other, to care for each other and to share more in the journeys of our cycles of life.

Is our evolutionary direction being guided and directed by a greater creative intelligence than we have yet come to completely know and understand. Have we been forced by the primal compulsions of our animal nature, to walk down the road of greed and its many destructive elements. Is this genuinely something that we could have avoided, or something that we will collectively be able to find a way out of and then learn from? It would be nice to have clarifying answers to all of these questions, and maybe, as more intelligent human beings, we might begin to get some more definitive answers. But for now, to bring each of us back to where we individually stand in this present moment of time, then we each only know what we know from our own unique experiences and perspective. To know something to be true for ourselves, we have had to reach that realisation upon our own contemplations and merits; if the knowledge or ideals are enforced or borrowed, then they belong to another, and we will still have to make up our own mind at some point, to become truly certain of our own perspectives.

And so it is that the explorations of this chapter are merely questions and ideas, hopefully to help to stimulate others in their own imaginations and contemplations, as we each have this gift and ability to travel and explore through consciousness. For me personally, then the real frontiers of human evolution ahead of us lie in the discoveries and expansions of our consciousness, which I believe are intrinsically linked to the expansions and explorations of outer space and all of its potentially abundant life. The physical Universe we live within is the living representation of the wider universal creative consciousness, ever evolving and exploring its infinite imagined possibilities; but that's just my belief and perspective and we on Earth are just one of its explorations. The more immediate questions before us all are, what of our more immediate future here on Earth: after all of the conflict of our history and the challenges of our modern world, how might we live and evolve beyond these preoccupations and their primitive impulses?

First of all, what might our societies actually look like when free of all the current inequalities and conflicts. We have no way of knowing where our population levels will be after all of the changes that lie ahead of us, but I am of a glass half full mind, so I would always naturally lean towards optimism, even if the odds were against us. With our new focus and motivations first being recovery from all of the excesses and destruction of years of capitalist greed and pollution, then building the new foundations of our world's infrastructures and economics will be paramount to achieving some initial stability, that can then be gradually built upon. If we start with the principle foundations of all energy production, industry and transport being based on clean sustainable energy, all food production being based on soil improving crop rotations, permaculture and organic farming methods, and all building being based on clean renewable materials, energy efficiency and longevity… then time and investment in these will establish an extremely solid foundation.

The biggest transitions will be in redirecting all of the budgets and labour previously involved in unsustainable and polluting industries and in the military and weapons production, into new clean and sustainable industries, and into the infrastructure investments and improvements that are needed for complete sustainability. The essentials for life are the main areas to invest in and improve first: clean water sources worldwide; strong rotations of food production with good local productions utilising techniques such as vertical planting, controlled irrigation and greenhouse production, but also with strong support networks across the globe; and good energy efficient homes and communities, with good sanitation, education and public transport networks. These are, of course, just some of the basics, but if these are all strongly invested in and continually reinvested in, to improve them year upon year, then they provide a secure foundation for all other social elements to flourish.

How we create and control money and finance to enable people the freedoms of trade and commerce, will need to change and evolve to become fairer and more directly practical. People in the present seem to forget that at some point in history we made up and created all of these systems of finance and economics; we choose how to print and circulate money to best suit our aims. From simple coin currency for direct trade, to the gold standard of the late 19th and 20th centuries, to the growing array of credit and digital moneys and fractional reserve banking. All of these now highly complex systems of finance were human made, that have evolved to allow private ownerships and controls of money, and the subsequent siphoning off of money and wealth for personal profiteering. Monetary systems can quickly become more simplified and honest again when all profiteering and private ownership is removed, they can then simply work for all people and their need for direct trade in day to day living, locally and internationally.

We certainly don't need money to live, as we cannot eat it or build homes with it directly; our essential stability lies in strong foundations of food production and water systems, and in good infrastructures of homes and communities, and when these are the priority investments of people within society, then money becomes just a simple medium for trade again. Public finance systems and community banks, non-profit making and completely structured to serve the people, would not be able to control and dictate our economics, they would merely facilitate them to function and grow between all regions and nations. Many community banks already exist, they are currently just dwarfed by the larger controls of the private banking companies.

Most of this chapter is based on what you might describe as idealism; we are looking at a theoretical world of humanity, living and working together as one completely cooperative species, now intelligent enough to realise that this is where its greatest strength lies. As people are inspired to work in cooperation, then they can create and build anything for their betterment, once they have a sustainable base for survival. As has been pointed out previously though, we already have all of these environmentally friendly and sustainable technologies in use and development within our current societies. So when we are able to remove the primitive conflicts of competition and greed, then all of these positive humanitarian and environmental technologies might be easily enabled to fully flourish, and to be given our full attentions and investments.

It's not such a huge step as you might first think, or as naive a possibility as it first might seem. Dreamers and idealists have been around since human contemplation first began, offering visions of utopian societies, none of which could be realised in the harsher realities of human fears, greed and conflict. The difference is, in today's reality with all of the growing pressures on our systems of survival, we are literally being forced to make a choice by the repercussions of our own actions: to work together or to fall apart, unity or selfishness, life or death. But then there is that part about removing the greed and conflicts of our current human nature; perhaps evolution is naturally allowing us down a path, a very difficult and challenging path, to ensure that this is actually what transpires, to ensure we cannot continue to make the same mistakes, to ensure that new more intelligent instincts become ingrained within us, and enable us to collectively move forwards in our evolution.

The instincts of our human nature are naturally at the very centre of this whole reality and all of the possibilities of our transition. This is about the priorities of our most dominant instincts; what we allow to direct us and how we interact with the world around us. Nature is a world of contrasts, as it has always been both beautiful and brutal: brutal in its raw geological power, in the predatory cycle of its food chains and in its indifference to death… yet often beautiful in its colourful displays of diversity, in the temporal nature of our vitality, and in the brief moments of blossoms and flowering, soon to be swept into diminishing memory and forgotten.

How we perceive these elements, the beauty and the brutality, and which is most prominent in our thoughts, is often in the eye of the beholder and the balance of the paths of our personal experiences; whether they are more harsh or gentile in their treatments. But with our expansion of consciousness and understanding of time, we have been given the ability to understand and appreciate all of nature's cycles, and the opportunity to adapt to and interact with these, to enjoy all of their diversities and contrasts. If we personally choose beauty over brutality, then we have the potential to enhance and support nature and all of its environments, and perhaps to truly feel for and understand nature and life to a much greater depth. I would like to believe that a more intelligent human being would mean we become less of an animal, caught up in the brutalities of survival, and more custodians of the planet, working with all of nature's powerful energies and beauties, progressing these and maintaining the balances of all of its diverse eco-systems.

I believe our minds are a medium for the very real energy of our consciousness. This energy is alive, it is sensitive, imaginative and creative, it is where all of the concepts and ideas first originated for everything that we have built in our technologically advanced world. My own questionings to life have led me to understand that consciousness holds the common identity between us all: without consciousness we are neither human nor actively alive. Technically you can be alive without consciousness, but there will just be a motionless bodily organism, no expression and no ability to communicate. What makes us human and each individually unique, is how we live through that genetically evolved organism: what character develops, what energy we project, how we think and express ourselves, how we imagine and create, how we learn to survive and how we cooperate and coexist. These are the energies and expressions of our own individual creative consciousness; this is what defines us as being alive.

My own personal and life long interests have always been very much aligned with how our consciousness is continuing to develop and evolve; what can we become and what will a more intelligent human being look like. Study for me has always been about the human condition, as we are all its living subjects and observers, and we all have the internal workings and instincts to be able to research and understand our nature in the reality of our own life's experience. This is how this book has come to be written; words drawn from the ether of consciousness, attempting to create, connect and share a message.

If we were able to take all of the human energy and ingenuity that is currently channeled into fear, conflict, commercialism, over complicated financial systems, and daily struggles for survival, then just imagine the potential we would have with the positive redirection of all of this energy, of billions of people. With an eventual solid foundation of super stable, clean and efficient social systems and communities, all of our energies will be free to flow into the further developments of our consciousness and all of its creativity: possible new ways to produce and work with energy, new ways to connect and communicate with each other and our environments, and new motivations to explore space and to try to understand the nature of the universe more. The mind has a huge untapped potential to deepen our understanding of what life actually is, all it requires is the time and energy to be free to question and explore.

These are just few simple suggestions, but whatever humans have dedicated consciousness and energy to we have quickly developed and progressed, and when new channels are explored, then many new thoughts and ideas can emerge. It is the branching nature of evolution to expand and explore every available channel and every door that is opened, which is a fundamental purpose and flow of all life here on Earth. Just take a look at the technological advances and developments of the last few decades. These have all come about because we have freed up time and energy, and invested these in huge projects of research and development. If we aim all of this time into social and environmental improvements, as opposed to it going into developing merchandise to generate personal profits, then just imagine the advancements that could be made in a short space of time. The unknowns of the untapped resources of our minds, and the unanswered questions about the source and nature of all life in the universe are just there, waiting for us to invest our time and energy.

How we could progress into our future will always be an unknown until we commit to explore new directions, like the conquering of the fear of fire and the first human explorations into new lands and environments; it is an unquestionable potential for us all as a race to move beyond fear and to come together and flourish. How would you choose to invest your energy if your time and thoughts were freed up completely? What would you like to see grow and develop in our world? Where do your deeper thoughts and questions to life take you to and look forward to? Given completely free reign, what is the ultimate type of world you would like to imagine and live within, in relation to the potentials that this planet currently offers us? Surely this is what creation gifted us imagination for, surely, if we invest in our visions, it allows consciousness and energy to flow there, and has the potential to become a reality. As always, it is your decision whether or not to explore further.

The world we live in today seems a long way from a united and fully cooperative human race instinctively supporting each other, as opposed to fearing each other, but we have to invest in such a world to begin to make it a reality. For some time we have had our agendas for society fed to us by those in control, often disguised as being for the benefit of all, but in reality, as this whole book has sought to highlight, they have been supporting greed psychologies and spreading them throughout human thinking. If we can remove greed from its positions of government and control over our world, and then focus all of our time and energy on building new clean and sustainable foundations to our societies, and to establishing simple and fair economies where there is no capabilities for profiteering… then it genuinely would not take more than a few decades to totally transform our world towards these idealistic visions. We have a long way to go and a lot of work ahead, but these visions and their potentials really are not that far away.

An optimistic and positive perspective on our possible future, is far better than no future at all. All of these transitions are already in their early stages and are genuinely possible, with room for our own unique diversities and beliefs to be incorporated. I am not predicting exactly how things might transpire, or the type of world that will exist in 20-30 years time; equal and fair cooperative societies can never be dictated or enforced upon us, and history has repeatedly proved that this will never work. This essential transition away from the destructive and unsustainable processes of greed, only works through the freedoms and equalities that allow for genuine collaboration and a united consensus to cooperate and support each other, in all of our challenges and endeavours. This is where our greatest strength and potential lies…, this, is true intelligence.

Only time will tell how we decide to face up to the greed in our world and all of the challenges it is presenting us with; this future, is in the hands of us all, and we each have a part to play.

Printed in Great Britain
by Amazon